Stacy

Best of luck
with everything! Let
me know how things
are going!

Love

Fred

How To Quit Working

A no-nonsense guide to replacing your income with what you KNOW instead of just getting PAID for what you do.

Jeff Steinmann

DEDICATION

This book is dedicated to everyone who is living a life that doesn't give them the FREEDOM to pursue the things that are most important to them.

You deserve better.

I did it and you can too.

Don't stop trying until you get what you want.

ABOUT THE AUTHOR

Jeff Steinmann has never accepted the fact that you can't always have what you want in life. As a kid, he thought that grown-ups got to do whatever they wanted; and at nearly 40 years of age, he has not given up that idea.

After several failed attempts at entrepreneurship, Jeff gave up on being an entrepreneur and his dream of a lifestyle of freedom and pursued a career in technology project management. Jeff quickly rose through the ranks of the technology departments of four major US Financial Institutions, ultimately managing the website conversions for the largest financial institution mergers in the U.S.

While he had great success in the corporate world, it simply didn't give him the freedom he always desired. After resigning himself to the fact that he would work a corporate job until retirement, he fell into a deep depression – he had given up on having the life of freedom that he always wanted.

He felt stuck because he just didn't know how he would ever gain the independence he wanted so badly without the traditional high risk of starting a business. Quitting his job, mortgaging his house, and just hoping for the best (all while hearing that 90% of businesses fail the first year) just didn't make a bit of sense.

Jeff searched high and low for a solution.

After devouring business books for two years, he finally discovered that the key to the lifestyle and success he wanted was to shift his thinking away from getting paid for what he DOES to making money from what he KNOWS. Knowledge and information can be written down, recorded, and packaged so it can be delivered without requiring his time to market, sell and deliver.

As he contemplated what expertise he could monetize, he asked himself an important question, "What do people ask you about?" The answer was clear. Jeff had rehabbed two houses and people frequently sought out his help on their Do It Yourself home improvement projects.

Jeff set out on a multi-year journey to figure out HOW to get himself KNOWN as an expert so he could package and sell his knowledge. He found hype and false promises from multi-level marketing companies, internet marketers and numerous others who claimed they had the formula, system, strategy or blueprint for making tons of money with your knowledge. After several false starts and many mistakes, Jeff nailed it. He finally figured out how all the pieces went together.

Along the way, Jeff became so knowledgable about the process of getting known for your knowledge that people started asking for his help. Then they started offering to pay him. Jeff knows an opportunity when he sees one, so he founded Braveau Experts. Braveau Experts partners with experts to get them known, build a following, and create products and programs.

Jeff has stripped away all the hype and B.S. and assembled only the best, proven, and most effective methods that have been used by all the most successful experts and gurus into a system he calls The Lifestyle Masterplan™ – a step-by-step guide to using your knowledge to build a business around your life. It's just like building a skyscraper, you start by cementing a solid foundation, erecting a strong structure of followers and finally raising the spire by selling products and programs that are practically guaranteed to sell. It is a step-by-step, no-hype, easy-to-follow system; and it works. It is not a "business opportunity" or "get rich quick" scheme; but rather, a proven system that incorporates only the best techniques used by the most successful experts and gurus.

His extensive knowledge of marketing, sales, business strategy and the application of technology, combined with his experience building expert businesses for clients and himself have made him a sought after consultant to experts and gurus at all levels of their businesses worldwide. Jeff works one-one-one with a small number of hand-selected clients each year, but primarily he works with clients through his group programs and online products.

He knows that many people want a life of freedom, but too often are lured into the false hopes and "get-rich-quick" promises of internet marketing, multi-level marketing, and work-from-home programs.

Today, Jeff lives the life of his dreams, working from his dream home in St. Louis, Missouri with a small international team. He works on his own schedule, when, where, how and with whom he wants. He enjoys helping people around the world use what they know to create the life of their dreams.

CONTENTS

Introduction

My Story

"The things I am giving up today are positioning me to have more of those things tomorrow."
— Jeff Steinmann

I have no idea how old I was, but I'm guessing I was 10 or 12. I distinctly remember sitting in a restaurant with my family. I was bored, as kids usually are when they are being forced to sit at a restaurant while the grown-ups gossip or talk about politics or the news. To put it in perspective, this was when kids were expected to be quiet. If they were bored, they had to deal with it, unlike today's kids who have handheld video games and a whole bag of toys to entertain them.

Being bored as ever, I started looking around at the number of waiters and waitresses in the restaurant. I speculated as to how much they might be getting paid. Then I looked at the space and wondered how much rent the restaurant paid. I thought about how the restaurant owners had to buy all the food and then pay someone to cook it. I wondered if the owners were getting some kind of deal because they ran a restaurant. Then it occurred to me — there is an entire kitchen that I can't see, and who knows how many people are working back there. Then I looked at the prices on the menu and roughly calculated how much the restaurant was making off of our table. I saw how many tables there were, did the math, and promptly decided the restaurant couldn't possibly be making money!

I thought about things like that A LOT as a kid. I was always trying to figure out how businesses worked, looking at them from the outside in. I tried to figure out how the heck they were making any money, and what their business was all about. I didn't think about this habit of mine because it was something I always did. I continued doing it as I got older, only my estimations and numbers got more accurate. Actually, reflecting back on that dinner I had with my family, I was totally right – the restaurant business sucks!

School Wasn't A Good Fit

I hated school — every bit of it. I remember in second grade when we were learning how to add and subtract big numbers, like 345 + 320. I would have an entire page of those equations to solve and I would sit, staring at the page, thinking that having to do all those math problems was the worst thing ever. I had much more important

Today I understand the importance and utility of math, but I certainly didn't in first grade. And I still don't think that having a 7-year-old do 35 addition and subtraction problems is a remotely effective way of teaching.

(fun) stuff to do! I had all kinds of little projects — the last thing I wanted to learn was something that had absolutely no practical application in the everyday life of a 7-year-old!

This hatred of formalized "learning for the sake of learning" continued into high school and college. I hated every second of "learning for the sake of learning." I didn't want to LEARN; I wanted to DO! Now when it came to DOING something, if LEARNING was required, it was no problem — as long as I had a REASON for learning what I was learning.

Failed Business Attempt #1

My college career was a 13-year journey to get a bachelor's degree. I bounced from college to college, full-time to part-time, major to major. Somewhere around the fifth year, I quit. It was the first time I actually made the explicit decision to quit school. I quit so I could pursue a project — to focus full-time on writing a book. I was working at the time and doing fairly well financially, mostly because I was making good money, living within my means and doing a great job of keeping track of my personal finances.

So what would I write about? I wanted to write a book about personal finance. The thing that would make my book unique was that I would write about how to use *Microsoft Money* to manage your finances. Not actually how to use the software, but how to make the software work for you as part of a holistic plan for your finances. I felt skilled and knowledgeable since that's what I was doing at the time with my own finances, and it was working well for me. I noticed that there were people teaching how to manage money, and people teaching about how to use the software, but no one was teaching *how to manage your money using the software*. I saw this as an unmet need in the market.

That was over 15 years ago, and in retrospect it was an awesome idea that, to my knowledge, hasn't been done yet. Great idea, right? Well, no. I didn't sell millions of copies of that book because in order to sell *any*, I would've had to actually write it!

I started by writing a few chapters and I distinctly remember why I quit. I quit because I was doing research and learned that the next version of *Microsoft Money* would be coming out in a few months. I decided that it would be too difficult to keep a book updated to correspond with the annual releases of software. In hindsight, that was a silly reason to not write the book. What was important were the concepts, not the details of the latest software version. But at the time, my vision was not big enough to see the reality of the situation. While I could come up with the concept for a book, I couldn't view it in the proper perspective to understand what was important.

Failed Business Attempt #2

My next attempt at entrepreneurship occurred when I was working a full-time job that was paying very well (thanks to the dot-com era, I was able to do this without a college degree, which I hadn't completed yet). I was still living within my means, saving money regularly, and doing all the right things. I was working for a major brokerage firm as a computer programmer. I worked on the website that clients used to view their accounts online. (We take it for granted now, but this was a revolutionary concept at the time.) I was on top of the technology of the day. I was working on a large, complex website that was accessed tens of thousands of times per day and had major security considerations. I really knew the technology well and felt like I could do anything (and I could have...from a technology standpoint).

In those days, actually selling something on the internet was incredibly difficult and expensive. You had to hire a team of programmers that no small company could afford. At the time, the technology was so complicated that a small company wouldn't even understand it well enough to hire the people needed to make it happen. I not only understood the technology, but with my ability to communicate and engage people, I also understood how to make it accessible to clients.

I set out to close this gap. I wanted to bring e-commerce to the small mom-and-pop business. I had documentation, a great plan; I knew how the technology was going to work; I researched the logistics of accepting credit cards online — the whole nine yards. I wasn't sure how I was going to sell the thing, but I was pretty sure I'd figure that part out.

I was fired up about my idea and also getting burned out with my job as a computer programmer. I was doing well financially and was living very inexpensively. It seemed like the perfect time to take a leap — to finally start my own business. I remember belaboring this decision. I went for long walks to think about it and try to figure out if it was the right thing to do. Would I fail? Would I succeed? What if I did fail? Finally I decided I was on the right track and was ready to make the leap. It was early 2001 when I set up an appointment with my boss for Thursday morning at 8:00 AM.

The night before the meeting, I was awake all night trying to feel more comfortable with my decision. Finally I sat down in the room with my boss — the moment had arrived.

I completely chickened out.

I made up some silly excuse about why I had asked for the meeting, and went back to my job.

No Regrets

I want you to know, I don't live with regrets in my life. I have made good decisions, bad decisions, and everything in between. I can honestly say that I don't look back on things and *wish* I had acted differently.

However this particular situation is the closest I have come to having regret. While the rational side of me knows that things worked out well for me, it is a decision I occasionally reflect on and wonder how it might have turned out differently.

I clearly remember the feelings I had after that meeting with my boss — I had pushed all this down inside and told myself it was going to be OK, that I would be fine working a corporate job until retirement.

Suckling On The 'CORPORATE Teat'

At that moment in time, I realized I was addicted to what I call the "corporate teat," to the security of my corporate job. I was like a baby bird whose mother kept feeding him worms. Why would I try to fly? I had (or so I thought) everything I needed. I had the security of a paycheck. I had the opportunity to move up. I had earned promotions in the past, so I knew how to do it.

But then I stopped moving up; I stopped getting better at my job because it was no longer a challenge. I knew exactly what I had to do to improve and be promoted. As a result, work was no longer a challenge for me. Most importantly, it would never offer me what I really wanted in life:

FREEDOM.

Freedom

I wanted the freedom to cut my own path — the freedom to make my own way without riding on the "tracks" of Corporate America. When you are working for a company (particularly a large one), you can go as far as you want, but it's like driving a train — you can only go where the tracks lead you. On the other hand, if you are an entrepreneur, it's like driving an ATV — you can go wherever you want. You can go over bumps; you can even go across the tracks. ATV's don't do well in water, but the great thing about being an entrepreneur is that if you want to go in the water, you can go get a boat. Or suit up and jump in. Or design an ATV that you can drive in the water!

That FREEDOM was what I was after.

Despite my big "chickening out" incident and the subsequent realization that I was addicted to the corporate teat, I continued working in the corporate world another ten years. I had a passion and drive to succeed and did well in that environment, delivered large technology projects successfully, and gained respect for being able to do so.

I learned invaluable skills in how to work with people, and figured out how to get people with different viewpoints, goals and perspectives on the same page and working toward the same goals.

However, as a project manager the most important thing I learned was how to:

MAKE STUFF HAPPEN.

Getting things done is a skill that few people master. It think it should be a required course in college — maybe grade school — to learn how to take a concept or idea to completion. If everyone had project management, or "getting stuff done," skills, we would accomplish amazing things in this world. People would be able to make their great ideas and dreams a reality — but that's another book (literally).

DO IT.

Unsuccessful people are not dumb; they are not without great ideas; they are not without passion; they are not typically lazy. They just didn't DO IT like successful people did. DOING IT is how you become successful.

DO IT — don't just talk about it; don't just plan it; DO IT.

Knowing how to DO IT has been the biggest key to my success.

Bye, Bye Corporate America

During the first part of my ten years in Corporate America, I had myself convinced that corporate life was working for me — that I would ride that train to retirement. After all, I was moving up, learning and growing; it was working for me, right?

The nature of project management (and one thing I loved about it) was that you didn't work on the same thing all the time. Projects had a finite beginning and end. You'd finish one and quickly move on to another.

Well the day came when I finished a project and (due to the company's priorities and the business conditions at the time) there wasn't another project for me to immediately start on. I had grown accustomed to moving on to a new project even before the previous one had ended, so this was quite a shock. Management told me they had several opportunities in the pipeline for me and that one would be available soon. They clearly understood that I thrived on challenges, and were doing their best to make an opportunity available that would allow me to grow.

Due to a series of unfortunate events, it took nearly eight months before I was assigned to a project.

Somewhere in those eight months, my passion for everything about my corporate career died.

It was a miserable time. I felt worthless, betrayed, and that I had worked hard only to be discarded. In truth, none of those things I was feeling were accurate. I was not being discarded; I wasn't useless; I wasn't worthless. In fact, on the contrary, management viewed me as so valuable that they worked hard to ensure I would get an opportunity to be stretched and challenged, and therefore be happy.

After eight months, I was assigned to a project — and boy was it a challenge. In fact, it was the most challenging project I had ever been involved with. There were technology problems, people issues, and political quagmires — literally every kind of challenge you could imagine.

And while management had presented me with a great challenge, there was one problem. Remember my passion had died sometime in the eight months before?

It wasn't for lack of trying, and it wasn't for lack of effort, but I did NOT rise to the challenge because the previous eight months of boredom and of not being challenged had left me too broken to perform. I had lost nearly all my confidence so I approached this project terrified of failure. I was fearful because I knew I badly needed to succeed. But regardless of the reason, I approached it in a way that was not successful.

I was replaced as the project manager and given a smaller role. It was devastating. I had built up my pride and my idea of who I was as a person around my corporate identity. When I failed at this latest project, I felt broken and without the confidence and self-assurance that I needed to perform well.

A New Opportunity

Then another twist. . .the Midwest-based, family-oriented company I worked for was acquired by a larger national company.

Everyone who worked there was devastated. Except me. :) Being disillusioned with my job and career, I saw it as an opportunity to start anew. This was my chance to start over and get back in my groove. I knew there were two potential outcomes:

1. I would be terminated, get a severance package and get a job with another company,

OR

2. I would keep my job (or a similar one) and start fresh with the new, combined company.

I ended up keeping my job at the new, combined company. And while I did give it my all and tried my best to stay energized and excited, management at the new company had a completely different perspective than I did on...well, almost everything. Theirs was not a perspective that I liked or wanted to be part of. But I needed the paycheck, so I kept on going as best I could. I learned when to keep my mouth shut and when to speak up. And at times I let it fly. The growing was over; the energy was gone; it was now a tough corporate grind. That company was subsequently purchased by another, even larger company which brought more of the same.

Stuck In A Rut

I was dead and broken — done with the corporate world. All of these events helped me to realize how little control I had over my own destiny in that world. I saw that it would never allow me to grow like I wanted and needed to. It was too rigid of an environment and I could not spread my wings.

I felt sooo stuck. I NEEDED that job! I NEEDED that paycheck! What could I do? I had a mortgage, lots of bills, and I had become accustomed to a very comfortable lifestyle. It sucked.

Jeff was really bored at his job.

How was I going to start a business when I was juggling a full-time (and high-pressure) job, maintaining a relationship, and pursuing an active social life and some serious hobbies? The thought was overwhelming! What should I do? Quit my job and hope for the best? How can you do that when you are reading statistics that show up to 75% of new businesses fail in the first year? Was I supposed to just quit my job and HOPE that I'd be one of the 25% who made it past the first year in business? Oh, and it would probably require me to wipe out my savings. What a great thing to do when you are about to eliminate your only source of income...

Not to mention, I had a LIFESTYLE to support. I had a taste for fine wine, great food, nice clothes and I lived in a beautiful house. Yes it sounds superficial, and it was!

The situation seemed insurmountable.

The Light Bulb Goes On

I very distinctly remember reading in bed one night. Right then and there, I made the decision that I was going to figure this out.

It was no longer about IF I was going to go out on my own — it was WHEN I was going to do it. I didn't know HOW, but I decided at that moment that I WAS going to figure it out.

I had no idea HOW to figure this out, but I knew I would. I didn't even know how to begin to figure out how to figure it out! So I made the best decision of my life.

I READ.

Because the book I was reading at the time was what inspired me to figure things out, I figured reading would be a good path. I committed to reading one business book per month. And I did.

Leaning Into It

I read books on finance, marketing, business, social media, investing, just about anything you can imagine. This is what the big gurus call "leaning into it." That's a powerful concept. And it really works. I wish I had thought of it.

Then along came Information Marketing. I picked up Yanik Silver's book, *Moonlighting on the Internet*. As I was reading it in bed, I sat up and said, "Holy shit, this is it!"

No industry, profession or business has such low barriers to entry, such flexibility, and unlimited profit potential. None. Period.

Information Marketing is what would allow me to get started while I was still working full-time

Information Product: "It's when you take the knowledge inside your brain and publish it." Don't let the word "publish" scare you. It's cool. We'll talk more about that later.

AND would give me the potential to reach the amazing heights that I desired.

Success At Last

From that realization, my company, *Braveau Experts*, was born.

Now I knew WHAT I was going to do. I knew exactly HOW I was going to transition from my full-time job to becoming an independent entrepreneur. It was finally coming together. I would build this business on the side; then when I felt comfortable that it was stable and making money, I would quit my job and pursue it full-time.

I was beyond excited. Way beyond excited.

I knew that my company was going to work with people who had some expertise and would help them to get known for that knowledge and create products based on their expertise. The really cool thing is that today my company is successful, and still has that very same mission. The wording and positioning has evolved, but it's exactly the same concept that I came up with in bed that night.

I figured out WHAT I was going to do and HOW I was going to do it. I did, however, realize and come to accept that there were going to be sacrifices. There would be things I would have to give up. I had a hard time accepting that at first. It changed for me when I realized that what I was doing was creating a lifestyle that would allow me to have much, much more of those things that I was choosing to give up temporarily now. It would give me MORE freedom to spend time with friends, MORE freedom to pursue hobbies, MORE money to have fine food and wine, and best of all, I would have the money to hire a personal trainer to help me stay in shape while eating all that fine food and wine!

When it comes down to it, one of the things that gets me the most excited is the idea of having the freedom to help friends when they need something, to volunteer for non-profits, etc. Money is awesome, but it gets boring very quickly. It's what you can DO with money and the quality of life you can create with it that are exciting.

How Do You Get Started?

I figured before I could do this for other people, I should give it a try for myself. I needed to publish my first information product. I would, as I had learned, start with what I knew. At the time, my biggest hobby was working on my rundown house that was built in 1916. I absolutely loved the architecture and the process of making it look new again, while still keeping the original character it had in 1916. I had previously rehabbed a house and made a considerable profit when I sold it. I thought, duh, this is what I know, so this is what I'll create information products on!

Cool, huh? I had been reading about how easy this stuff is. All you have to do is hiccup and it will go viral, right??!!! I thought, I've got the skills to get a website up; I can do a blog; I can do Facebook and Twitter; I can shoot some video; I can create some products – no problem. All I have to do is do it.

Wrong. Wrong. Wrong. Totally wrong. It doesn't work that way! What I found was a lot of tactics, ideas and concepts. I did NOT find the elusive magic or silver bullet. My new business didn't take off as fast as everyone had promised.

Shifting Into Gear

At this point, I was getting my education from free information on the Internet or $10-20 books I'd buy online or at the bookstore. I finally had a bit of a shift. I realized that I was going to have to invest in myself and my education. And by invest, I mean pony up thousands of dollars for training, coaching, mentoring, etc.

Fortunately, since I was working a full-time job making good money and had a solid savings account, I could afford to make those investments. I will never forget when I bought my first $1997 training product. It was a scary decision, but one I NEVER regretted. I kept going, eventually investing in several products and programs; however, the most invigorating and best parts were the live events I had access to. I met lots of great people, learned a lot, and most of all became very INSPIRED!

As I attended these events and trainings, I found that when I explained what my company was going to do (and it was just a concept at the time) people were very excited and intrigued! They were asking for my help in droves. In fact, people were *approaching me* for help in building their expert lifestyle business. I realized that I was on to something.

The Missing Piece

Things were going well from an educational/inspirational standpoint, but I was growing somewhat frustrated. I knew I was on the right track, but something wasn't quite right. I won't call it an epiphany, but I will call it a long, slow realization. The bottom line was that everything I was doing was either a high-level strategy OR a low-level tactic — and they were not connected or working together cohesively.

Here is what I noticed — all of the training I was receiving, whether expensive, mid-range or cheap, taught one of two things:

A) High-Level Strategies
OR
B) Low-Level Tactics.

Not one program was teaching an end-to-end plan that would incorporate the tactics with the long-term strategies, and create a structured business. This is the piece that was missing — a long-term strategy <u>with</u> integrated tactics.

The Lifestyle Masterplan™

Realizing what I needed was TOTALLY AWESOME! Here's why. I knew exactly how to create plans that integrate tactics and strategies — I had been doing it for years as a project manager! Now that I knew WHAT I needed to do and I knew HOW to do it, it was going to be easy.

My corporate experience gave me everything I needed to take all this information I had learned and put it together into a comprehensive, end-to-end methodology or system. How cool! The Lifestyle Masterplan™, was born. We'll get into the details of it later.

The Turning Point

At the time of my realization, I was still working my full-time job...disillusioned as ever. In fact, now that I had something that excited me, I was even more disillusioned with my corporate job. Then came a turning point. It happened on a flight from San Francisco to Chicago. And it was a big one.

I was reading Timothy Ferriss' *The Four-Hour Workweek*. I was already familiar with the concepts, and based on reading the back cover and a few reviews, I was not interested in reading the book. But it seemed to have so much applicability to what I was doing and was so popular, that I felt like I needed to read it. So I started reading.

For some reason, when I read I HATE doing the exercises at the end of each chapter (on the other hand, as an author I feel it's irresponsible not to include them!)

Despite this, I did one of the exercises in the *Four-Hour Work Week*. Starting on page 46 of the revised version, there is an exercise called "Questions and Actions" which I did. Tim designed that exercise to help you work through your fears about making a leap or change, i.e. leaving your full-time job. My verbatim responses to his questions are below.

Questions & Actions Exercise

Question) What is the absolute worst thing that could happen?

Answer) I quit my job and do not make any money. I cannot pay the mortgage and the house is repossessed. I do not have any money and have to move in with someone. I have no insurance and get sick, with no money, and some illness is worse because it goes untreated. I borrow money from friends to pay medical bills. I no longer can afford to keep Frankie (my dog) and have to give her up. I become severely depressed and cannot afford psychiatric care.

If I have no job, I will be able to spend a great deal of time on my business making an income. More than likely I will be able to afford at least some sort of catastrophic health coverage. I can always work at Starbucks just for the health insurance.

Question) What steps could I take to get things back on track if this worst-case scenario happened?

Answer) I could get a contracting job probably pretty easily which would get me insurance and a good salary. Working a lower-level job would also be a good option to get health insurance. I will have the seed of an income stream before this, so I will not be starting from scratch. I can always move into an apartment building I own at a low cost. If I lived with a friend I could do work at their house in lieu of rent. I could create fast information products or do consulting for small businesses for some additional income.

Question) What are the most likely outcomes, good and bad?

Answer) I will have to cut back on unnecessary expenses. It may be a little rough. I will probably run up some credit card debt. I will likely dip into savings and have to do with less financial resources for my business.

I will be incredibly fulfilled and really enjoy the freedom and focus on my business. I will be able to focus on growing my income and get into a regular entrepreneurial routine which will only serve to make me happier, more motivated and ultimately more successful.

It is highly unlikely that I can't produce at least a decent income to live off of. Much less intelligent people have done this.

Question) If I were fired today, how could I get back on track?

Answer) I would simply go interview with contracting firms and while it may take some time, I will find a job contracting. If not, I will use all these new skills I have gained to pick up consulting gigs or something like that. I can also cut spending WAY back and live very simply.

Question) What do I fear the most and what is the worst outcome?

Answer) I fear telling some friends and family what I am doing because they won't understand or will belittle me. The worst that can happen is that they won't understand or they will belittle me. I heard many successful entrepreneurs say that was just their experience. They seem to be doing fine.

Question) What is the inaction costing you?

Answer) It is prolonging my unhappiness and preventing me from getting to my dreams faster. I have a LOT I want to do and need to get started because I'm not getting any younger. I got this close to quitting my job and starting a business ten years ago, but I chickened out. I can't really say I regret that because the experience I got in the past ten years will be a key to my success. But I won't chicken out this time.

Question) What are you waiting for?

Answer) I want to balance taking risk with being practical. June will be a great time as I will have a nice cushion then and a good starting income stream. So I am waiting for June.

The Commitment

After going through the exercise, I made a decision, a very big decision. It was November. I made the decision right then and there that I was going to leave my full-time job about seven months later. I'm not exactly sure why I chose that date, but I think it was because it was a little more than six months out and I felt like that was about the right amount of time to build more momentum with my business. Based on my financial situation, I knew I could make it until the end of the year. That felt good because it gave me the security of knowing I had about 13 months to make money.

So there it was. I had made my decision. I knew there was one way that I could really make it stick:

TELL PEOPLE.

Telling people meant I would subsequently be subjecting myself to the humiliation of failure if I did not make my goal. What a fabulous and scary idea.

Making The Leap

I had not made the leap for YEARS because of one reason: I was afraid of failing. I was terrified that something would go wrong and I'd be poor, broke, etc. (See the *Four-Hour Work Week* exercise for Tim's response to these fears.) But now I linked my worst thought of pain to NOT TRYING, to NOT making the leap. I was honestly very, very afraid of that prospect.

I'm not suggesting you sit back, drink a beer, watch TV and wait for Ready to arrive. That won't work. (Besides, watching TV is a complete waste of time.) Ready will come if you "lean into it."

It was one day during a phone call when I had this abrupt realization. I have a great friend who I often confide in and whose opinion on financial matters I value. This was a situation where I needed to make a financial decision, and I was sort of struggling with it because of all I had going on at the time and the uncertainty that I was feeling about my scheduled June 30th departure from my full-time job. As my friend helped me to think through my options and the pros and cons of each, he asked, "What if you stayed at your job another two months or so?" Without a moment's pause, I snapped back, "Absolutely not! That is NOT an option." It was at that point that I realized what a true decision is. I had cut myself off from any other possibility. I was leaving my full-time job on schedule. NO MATTER WHAT.

Are You Ready?

I've made a few big decisions in my life. There are several that took a long time to make, like this one. The decision (and I mean REAL decision) comes when you are really Ready (that's ready with a capital R). Ready happens. Ready just happens when you least expect it. When you are Ready, you are Ready. The reason I was able to make the solid decision that I did is because I was Ready. I clearly knew that I wanted this ten years earlier. Why didn't I make the decision ten years earlier? I was not Ready then. But now I was Ready.

Lean Into It

For me, "leaning into it" meant reading every business book I could possibly get my hands on. . . and tolerate. I even read a book that was nothing but definitions of terms for 250 business and investing words. Yes, I basically read a business dictionary cover to cover! But I have no regrets. Maybe that wasn't the best choice of books, but the bottom line is my reading strategy worked. There is no magic formula or reading list that will work for everyone, but I'll gladly share the list of the books I read (and yes, they worked for me).

howtoquitworkingbook.com/booksiread

Virtual Mastermind Group

As I write this, I find myself quoting the big guru's / self-help folks. I don't recall how I got started reading and studying Tony Robbins, the late Zig Ziglar (I'm considering changing my name to Stein Steinmann — what do you think?), Brendon Burchard, Mark Victor Hansen, Eckhart Tolle, David Allen, Dan Kennedy, etc., but what I can say is:

THANK GOODNESS I DID!

Those guys kept me going — they were my virtual support team. This may sound hokey, but I could not have done it without my "Virtual Mastermind Group." As thoughts popped into my head or stuff happened in my life, I would frequently think about one of them. What would they tell me if they were a personal friend? What would Tony Robbins tell me to do with that "what if I fail?" thought in my head right now? What would Eckhart Tolle tell me to do with all the worry I feel? What would David Allen tell me to do when I feel out of control and overwhelmed with all I have to do?

One of the best things I did was to listen to motivational and inspirational books on CD while driving. That was a powerful use of "found time," and worked well for me. The time you spend driving is an opportunity to take in valuable new concepts. In fact, an abridged version of this book is available on CD. To get your copy, visit:

howtoquitworkingbook.com/cd

Leaving my corporate job to pursue my dream of having an expert lifestyle business has been even more incredible than I imagined it would be. I absolutely love it! There are so many people who are doing things that don't make them happy. After gaining all this wisdom from my Virtual Mastermind Group, I decided I needed to write a book. The bottom line is that I realized I have information in my head that can help a lot of people become happier, and I'm excited to share it with you.

The Benefit To You

I've spent $57,456 so far on educating myself and learning about the individual pieces of how to build an expert lifestyle business. It was money well spent, but what I really needed to know was how to put it all together into a complete business system. That's why I created The Lifestyle Masterplan™ and am sharing it with you now.

Enjoy it; use it to create your expert lifestyle business.

I'd love to hear about your success with The Lifestyle Masterplan™. Please email me at Jeff@TheLifestyleMasterplan.com to share your story.

Chapter 1

Design Your Life

"My definition of success is to live your life in a way that causes you to feel a ton of pleasure and very little pain — and because of your lifestyle, have the people around you feel a lot more pleasure than they do pain."

- Tony Robbins

It took me a while to figure this out. It actually took me quite a long time to realize that I only want one thing out of life – FREEDOM. When I was a child, I thought that grown-ups got to do whatever they wanted. When I got older, I found out that wasn't as true as I had thought...but I never gave up hope.

My idea of the best life possible is having the "space" to pursue it. That means being able to go after the things that make me happy, fulfill me, and make me absolutely the best person I can be.

When I took the Passion Test™ by Janet and Chris Atwood, I realized that the single most important thing in my life is to be the best I can possibly be. (What that means is the subject of another book!) In order to do that, I need freedom — freedom to be who I am, to do what I want to do, to make changes as I see fit.

As a practical matter, first and foremost, that means not being tied to a job or a business. It means being able to make decisions based on what I *want* out of life, not what will pay the electric bill next month.

The Income Obstacle

As I set out to launch my dream life and create that freedom, the very first obstacle I came across was money. I did not have enough of it to have the freedom to pursue life the way I wanted. This lack of money required me to sell my time, which is the most precious resource I have. Time is the resource that allows me to be what I want to be in life, but I needed money to put

> Time is ALL YOU HAVE. It is really the only resource that you cannot get more of. You can get more money, get more friends, learn more, etc. Time is the great equalizer.

food on the table and a roof over my head (to start with). The only way to get the money I needed was to sell my time. I had to sell the hours in my day to a company in order to get money. That's not my idea of free!

What I needed was money coming in on a regular basis, flowing into my bank account consistently, and funneling in regardless of whether I was selling my time or not. I recognized that this obstacle is not as much about money as it is about INCOME. I needed to create an income that NEVER required me to sell my time!

Making The Shift

Here is how I look at it. Let's say you have a machine that makes coffee cups. The machine costs you $45,000, which you borrowed to purchase it. It makes 100 coffee cups per day and can operate for 30 consecutive days. You can sell the cups for $10.00 each. Each cup requires $5.00 worth of clay, paint and other supplies to make. The labor to run the machine costs $2.50 per cup. If you run the machine at its maximum capacity and then use all your profit to pay back the loan, in six months you will be making a pure profit of $2.50 per cup. This is a simplified example, but stick with me.

Let's say you can dismantle that machine and sell it for parts totaling $150,000. In fact, you have someone standing in front of you right now offering you $35,000 just for the handle-maker.

What are you going to do? Should you sell him the handle-maker and make a fast $35,000?

Sure, if you want to give up the $90,000 per year in profit that you will make after you pay the machine off in six months. In those first six months, you won't make a dime — all your profits will go to pay back the loan. But after the first six months are over, how does $90,000 per year in profit sound?

When you sell your time for money, it's like selling your handle-maker. And while you might be selling it for a good profit, that profit pales in comparison to what you can make if you keep your machine intact and focus on building a money-making resource. Instead of selling off your assets (and then having nothing to use to make money), it's important for you to understand how to leverage your assets so they can make money for you.

As I thought about this, I decided to make a shift. I wanted to stop selling the hours in my day and start using my time to build a machine that makes coffee cups — no wait, I mean money! When I sell an hour of my day to someone else, I can make about 250 bucks. But if instead I use that hour to build passive income streams, I am putting things in place that will make money on an on-going basis, and will not require my daily hours to be used in the future. Rather I am building systems that continue to generate money day after day after day.

Time Is Your Only Asset

The only thing we have that is worth anything is time.

What do you, Oprah, Donald Trump, and the homeless guy on the corner all have in common? You each have 24 hours in a day. No one has more, no one has fewer.

You can get more money; you can get more resources, more education, more knowledge, more help, more friends, or more stuff. But you will never, ever get more than 24 hours in a day. It is the ONLY thing we have in life that is completely fixed — and how we use it determines how much we enjoy our lives.

How much I enjoy my life is my only measure of success. The most challenging part of my life has been FIGURING OUT what that means. What is it that makes me happy? I get closer to my answer each day, and the day I completely answer that question is the day I die.

Build A Machine That Makes Money

As you can see, the first thing I needed to do in order to launch my dream life was to build that money-making machine. I needed to get that thing built and cranking away. A little coffee-cup-making machine wasn't going to cut it either. I needed something much bigger.

Always look at the big picture. And when I say big picture, I mean BIG! The first thing I did (I remember getting this inspiration while I was running one day) was to create a really

BIG plan in my really BIG head, for a REALLY BIG MACHINE!

Have A Clear Strategy

I wanted to have a very clear strategy that would enable me to meet my financial goals. That strategy could be another book, but I can sum it up very simply:

I build businesses that make money which I then invest in real estate.

Real estate is my core business. Everything I do is to make money to invest in real estate. My profits from this book will be indirectly invested in real estate. All the money I make, directly or indirectly, goes into real estate. Real estate then provides the passive income I need to be free. Real estate is the best investment in the entire world. I don't care what anyone says about this real estate market, or that real estate market. It's simply the best thing you can ever invest in. Why? Because there is nothing else in the world that has such a completely fixed supply and such a certain demand. Of course, there will be ups and downs, but it will never go out of style and it will never go away. (Well it will all go away eventually, but we'll have bigger problems when that happens.)

Look At The Big Picture

In order to be massively successful, on the scale I intend to be, looking at the big picture is essential. It can be challenging because you have to be more concerned about three, five, ten or 20 years from now than you are about tomorrow. If you are more focused on how you are going to pay your next month's mortgage payment, or how you are going to put tomorrow's food on the table, you will end up making the next mortgage payment and putting the next meal on the table at the expense of your future. On the other hand, if you are more focused on the future, the next mortgage payment and meals will come. And more importantly, so will the future you planned for.

To be clear, when I say you should be more concerned about 20 years from now, I'm NOT saying you shouldn't live in the moment, or be present. You absolutely should! In fact, the more you are in the moment, present and enjoying your life, the less you will worry about tomorrow. And you will develop an even better plan for 20+ years from now.

If you are wondering how you can focus on the future while also being present in the moment and enjoying life, keep reading. That's where we're going next.

Do Something You Care About

I realized early on that this was gonna be a lot of damn work! There are many people out there with systems, programs, software, etc. who say they can make it less work; but I'm giving you the plain and simple truth — it's gonna be work. But don't get me wrong, it's TOTALLY worth it!

If I'm going to work hard at something, I better damn well enjoy it! More than enjoy, actually... That's why you have to pick something that you love and are passionate about. Don't choose a business because of the money it could make, the marketability, the prestige, the demand, or any of the other terrible reasons why people pick careers, start businesses or take a certain direction in life. Choose something that will have you excited to get up every morning and work at it. This is the only way you will be happy doing this.

My business was born out of my passion. Braveau Experts was designed very precisely to take the greatest advantage of my strengths and to get me doing EXACTLY what I want to be doing.

I'm obsessed with doing *what I want to do*.

Align The Business With Your Lifestyle

Align the business with the lifestyle you WANT, not the lifestyle you HAVE. If you want freedom to travel, make sure your business will give you that freedom. If you want lots and lots of money, make sure your business will provide that. If you want to be famous, you can do that too; just make sure you are the personality at the center of your business. If you love to write, make sure you get to write a lot in your business. We'll talk more about this in chapter seven.

I knew a few things about what my business would have to be. I understood the key points that were absolutely necessary to make it work for me, and that would keep my business in alignment with my goal of having the freedom to pursue what I want out of life.

Here are my key points:

1. *My business has to be scalable.* That means it has to be able to grow to an unlimited size and income potential. My business will constantly grow, and make huge amounts of money — more and more each year. I cannot do that with a company that requires a great deal of my time on an ongoing basis. Requiring huge amounts of my time to BUILD is OK, but requiring huge amounts of my time to RUN is NOT OK. There is only so much time that any person, no matter how dedicated or focused they might be, can (and should!) provide to a company.

2. *My Business has to be mobile.* I want to be able to work from anywhere. My business has to allow me to work with only a laptop, phone and internet connection. Today there is no reason to be tethered to an office. If I want to live in Egypt; I'll live in Egypt. If I want to live on an island in the South Pacific; I'll live on that island. If I want to live in St. Louis, Missouri; I'll live there. If I decide to move somewhere else, I want to be perfectly positioned to do so.

3. *My Business has to make me happy!* It has to be fun. I want to have a blast when I'm working! I know that I'm happy when I'm creating stuff — I have to be making or

building something. This business affords me the ability to be creative. If it were a business that was about repeating a process, such as installing garage doors, marketing consulting, software implementation or something like that, I could not be happy, because I wouldn't be building things. My company takes ordinary people who know a lot about something and teaches them to replace their income with what they know. I help people become well-known experts who have the ability to reach, touch and help massive numbers of people. The company that I built CHANGES LIVES every day. I love that.

I structured my business around what I want, and created a business I love. You can create businesses for any number of reasons, and structure them many different ways. My business is structured around the key things that I knew I needed in order to be happy. You'll create your ideal business based on the key things YOU need in order to be happy.

My Big Mistake

I got most of it right with Braveau Experts, but I did make a big mistake early on. It all came to a head one afternoon.

I had gone out to run errands that morning. Something really minor went wrong; I think my web host went down. That silly little issue completely pushed me over the edge. I was really frustrated and angry, and feeling generally stressed out and unhappy. When I got home I took a ceramic coffee cup and spiked it in the driveway, shattering it into a million pieces. And then felt like a complete idiot.

I had been frustrated for a while — which was particularly annoying because I was no longer working my corporate job! I was making great progress in my business and I THOUGHT I had everything I wanted. I should have been THRILLED.

As I sat down at my desk to continue working, I finally understood why I was so frustrated. I had built a business that was not completely aligned with what I wanted my life to look like.

Braveau Experts 1.0, as I'll call it, was basically an agency. We worked with people who wanted to become known for their knowledge and expertise, and we did everything FOR THEM. That meant we handled their technology, social media, content creation, products, etc., and they provided the creative and expertise.

It was a good and viable business model, but it was NOT good for me. It was not compatible with what I wanted MY life to look like.

I literally was working to help others (my clients) to live the lives THEY wanted, but had neglected what I wanted out of MY life!

Create Your Desired Life

That very afternoon I called all of my clients to let them know that I would no longer be offering the services I had been. I informed them that I would now be focusing on the part of my business that IS compatible with my goals, and enables me to live the life I want to live.

In other words, Braveau Experts would no longer do things *for* our clients; we would shift to a model of teaching and consulting.

That was the best decision I ever made. It was worth the shattered 1996 St. Louis Blues coffee cup!

What I learned from this was that I must KNOW and WRITE DOWN exactly what I want my life to look like. That means I have to be clear on things like, if and how much I want to travel, how many hours a week I want to work, the type of work I want to do, who I want to work with, and when I want to work.

When architects design a building, the first thing they do is create what they call an "Elevation View." An elevation view is simply a drawing of what the building looks like from the outside. They usually draw it from several perspectives, like the front elevation, rear elevation, side elevation, and so on. Do exactly the same thing for your expert lifestyle business. Start by drawing what you want your LIFE to look like!

It's easy to do because I developed the "Lifestyle Elevation View" — a document that prompts you with pinpointed questions about what you want your life to look like. There are many links throughout this book, but if you only visit one of the links, make it this one: howtoquitworkingbook.com/elevationview (By the way, it doesn't require *actual drawing,* so don't worry about that!)

Answer the questions and use the Lifestyle Elevation View to guide EVERY decision you make in your business. You may not be able to have everything exactly the way you want it right away, but you never will if you don't keep your ideal life in sight. Just like they do on a construction site, keep this document pinned up near your work area, so you can always see exactly what you want your life to look like. Then you can make each decision with your clear vision in mind.

Conclusion

You are reading this because you are setting out to use what you know to create an amazing life of freedom for yourself, and to help many people. That puts you among the bravest, coolest, and most influential people on this earth!

Keep reading. This is an exciting journey and I'm thrilled and honored to show you the path.

Think Of It Like This:

- ✘ Give serious thought to *exactly* what you want your life to look like.
- ✘ Don't settle for anything less than that. You can have it.

Do It Like This:

- ✓ Download and complete the Lifestyle Elevation View at howtoquitworkingbook.com/elevationview.
- ✓ Keep that document with you at all times and use it to guide every decision you make and everything you do – be ruthless about this.

Chapter 2

Make The Commitment

"If you had started doing anything two weeks ago, by today you would have been two weeks better at it."

— John Mayer

This is by far the scariest part of the whole process — when you actually decide to put all your faith in yourself. Now it's time to take the step that will make your dream life of freedom come true. This is also the *most important step* you will take.

What you are really doing is deciding to give up SOMETHING — maybe it's another business, a full-time job and the steady paycheck that comes with it, or perhaps it's some of the time you spend with family and friends. It will be different for everyone. Trust me — you do not have room for something this BIG to enter your life without letting something else go. You have to create the space in your life for this BIG new focus. You need to free up time, energy and resources so that you'll have them to apply to your new creation. However, letting go can be the scariest part.

It's usually not a small or trivial thing. For me, at first it meant letting go of a lot of hobbies, free time, and time with friends and family, because I started my business while I was working full-time. The next thing I had to give up was the security and paycheck of my full-time job. That was even harder!

It wasn't an easy decision, but I didn't struggle with it simply because I wanted the new lifestyle so badly. It helps if you realize that you are giving up some things temporarily, in order to have more of those things in the future.

Getting Ready

I made the leap because I was Ready. Let's start by defining what Ready is. It's not sitting on the couch drinking a beer, watching TV, waiting for Ready to magically appear. You get Ready. You lean into it.

That means taking as big of a step as you can at the time. It may mean starting with something as simple as reading this book. If that is your first step, congratulations, you made a very wise decision. I'm glad to be a part of it!

This may not feel easy and there is no magic formula. You have to put one foot in front of the other. I'll share some of the things that helped me to get Ready.

Am I Smart Enough?

I really wondered about this. I worried that I wasn't smart enough, dedicated enough, or even suited to this type of thing. I adopted a different perspective by watching people, particularly by observing other entrepreneurs. I saw that there are many successful entrepreneurs who do not appear to be as smart as I am, and who don't have the resources that I do. I am certainly not the smartest guy in the world, but I'm far from the dumbest. And there are many people, who fall below me on the "smart-meter," yet who have a great deal of success. As a result, I figured 'smartsies' shouldn't stop me, right? Right. It shouldn't stop YOU either. By leaning into it with a positive attitude, I learned that it isn't about how *smart* I am; it is about how *committed* I am.

Decisions Vs. Results

Try this: compare yourself to other entrepreneurs. Look at the differences between you and them. Really look. What separates you from them? Here are the types of things I want you to evaluate:

1. How hard do they work?
2. What risks do they take?
3. What did they give up in the beginning?
4. What type of people do they surround themselves with?
5. How do they view the world: positively or negatively?

These are the factors that enable you to build a successful business. And what's surprising to most people is that these are all DECISIONS. You DECIDE how hard you will work. You DECIDE what risks you will take. You DECIDE what to give up. You DECIDE who to surround yourself with. You DECIDE how you will view the world.

When you are looking at other entrepreneurs, here are some things I *don't* want you to look at:

1. How much money do they have?

2. What type of platform do they use? (How many people listen when they talk?)
3. What resources do they have — office space, staff, technologies, etc.?

I don't want you to look at these things, because these are RESULTS. They are the RESULTS earned from making good DECISIONS.

If you focus on other entrepreneurs' results, you may fall into the trap that so many get caught in of thinking, "I don't have enough money" or "I don't have a platform" or "I don't have an office, staff, and technology." But those are statements of results. Results come from getting the first things (the decisions) right.

Get the decisions right, and the results will come.

The Antiquated Concept Of A Job

I want to spend some time talking about jobs because the reliance on a job and perceived security of getting a regular paycheck are the major reasons people do not follow their dreams.

There is a prevailing mentality that your job is some sacred thing that can't be replaced, that losing your job is the worst thing that could happen. There is an awful, negative aura around losing your job. But the whole concept is totally out-of-whack. A job is ONE way to make money TODAY. There are always other jobs and, more importantly, *many other ways* to make money.

I need to talk about the economy. As of this writing, we are in the worst recession/depression (I'm not going to debate what to call it) of my lifetime, perhaps of the century. The Lifestyle Masterplan™ is about creating your OWN economy. Then you will no longer be required to participate in any economy. You will no longer care about how many jobs are available.

Congratulations, You Lost Your Job!

I congratulate people when they lose their job! Before I made the final step to leave my high-paying corporate job, I already had this perspective. I watched many friends and coworkers lose their jobs. I saw them devastated, but shortly afterwards they were in a BETTER job or a better situation. I don't know of any smart, ambitious, motivated person who has ever lost a job and ended up in a worse situation.

This *sacred job* mentality comes from the post-industrial revolution notion that it is the duty of an employer to take care of us and protect us by giving us health insurance, retirement, a guaranteed income, raises, etc. Before the industrial revolution, there was a much higher proportion of entrepreneurs. While the industrial revolution was a shift to a higher use of our intellect as human beings, it also had the negative effect of leading to a mentality of dependence on jobs. We began looking to our employers to take care of us.

Before, people didn't travel far regularly, since cars and roads weren't as prevalent as they are today. Folks shopped at their neighborhood grocery store, neighborhood butcher shop, cobbler, tobacco shop, bakery, and so on. All of these businesses were nearby and run by entrepreneurs. I'm not old enough to remember those days, but I doubt they called themselves *entrepreneurs*. Just like fish don't call water *water*, they see it as "their world." (I'm assuming here — I've never asked a fish!)

> Go to school and get good grades, so you can find a company to take care of you (read: be dependent on) until you retire. That's what grown-ups keeping telling kids. It's a horrible message to send to young people.

Empowered Or Disempowered?

When I worked in the corporate world, particularly toward the end when I was very disillusioned with the whole thing, I began to feel trapped. I felt like I NEEDED the company in order to survive and live. And I didn't like that feeling one bit — it was disempowering.

Now I understand that I crave independence, and to be in control of my destiny. I want to decide what I am going to do each and every day. I want to begin working because I want to work, not because it is Monday at 8:00 a.m. Right now, it is Monday at 9:55 a.m. and there is nothing else I'd rather be doing than writing this book — THAT is an empowering feeling!

Whose Goals Are You Reaching?

It worries me that we teach our children to become dependent on a corporate entity whose goals will NECESSARILY *never* match yours. I'm serious when I make that statement. The goals of a corporation NECESSARILY can never match yours.

A corporation is OWNED by shareholders. I don't care what they say, or what is in the corporate mission statement, a corporation's obligation is to their shareholders. Whether you like it or not, agree with it or not, it is fact. It is how it is. When it comes time to make decisions, the interests of the shareholders come first. That's how it is and how it should be. The shareholders OWN the company. It exists for *their* benefit, not the employees' benefit. It follows then, that when tough decisions have to be made, the shareholders' interests (i.e. profitability) will be chosen over any perceived need to take care of employees.

I don't want to have that arrangement as my *exclusive* way of making money. And it certainly is not what I call job security.

I'm not "hating" on corporations or the concept of legal entities. They provide good and necessary structures that enable commerce to occur in a way it could not otherwise and they benefit many people; however, we have developed unrealistic expectations of corporations when it comes to the idea of them taking care for us for 45 years.

What if you work for a non-profit? The main difference between a non-profit and a corporation is that the non-profit has responsibilities to the people they are chartered to serve, i.e. homeless kids, battered women or cancer patients. Those responsibilities also will NECESSARILY come before any obligations to employees. In the end, it's not really any different — the employees' needs come last.

Even if it is a different legal structure like a sole proprietorship, partnership, or family business, although there is less legal obligation and more flexibility, the interests of the sole proprietor, family or partners will generally come first — as it should.

Learning To Fly

This doesn't mean you should never work for another entity. You should! I learned 75% of my business and people skills from my 15 years of corporate experience. Working for a company is great when your goals are in alignment with theirs. There are times when the needs of an individual will match the needs of a corporation, and it works well and everyone is happy for a while. Is it likely that those needs will be in alignment for 45 years or more? Probably not. It's not a good strategy to latch onto that corporate teat for 45 years, expecting it to care for you until you die, and to care more about you than it does about its owners/shareholders. This just goes against all common sense.

Let's look at birds for a moment. A mother bird cares for her young until they are old enough to go out on their own. Then she pushes them out of the nest. They learn to fly after some difficulty, risk and a learning curve. But eventually they learn how to fly! (This is fresh in my mind as I just watched it happen on my front porch.) Mama bird cares for the babies until they are ready, then they are off on their own. Mama teaches them how to fly and how to find food. She does NOT tell them that they need to go find another mama bird to take care of them for the rest of their lives. She teaches them what they need to know so they can ultimately fend for and take care of themselves.

That is what entrepreneurship is all about — being able to fend for yourself, no longer being dependent on anyone else for your worms; you find your own worms. Trust me when I tell you that there comes a point when worms (business opportunities) *will come to you*. You actually won't be able to eat them all, as opportunity quickly outpaces your capacity for it. And boy is that a good thing!

The World Is A Plentiful Place

One of the things that helped me immensely after I made the leap was to maintain an attitude that there are an *unlimited* number of ways to make or get money. I don't worry about money because I know that if I need money, I will just go make it. Period.

This perspective is nothing more than a DECISION. That one decision completely changed how I looked at my situation. Imagine these two different viewpoints:

1. If this doesn't work, I will have to go get another job, or go beg for my old job back.

OR

2. If what I am currently doing doesn't work, I will adjust, change, reposition, redo or whatever I need to do. If I can't do that fast enough, I will consult, do odd jobs, or whatever I need to do in order to make it work.

I like #2 better — it is a more empowering perspective on life. And when you chose to think in those terms, you will relax a lot more. I know because I worried less — a lot less. In fact, I worried very little after I changed my mindset. I stopped worrying because I had made the commitment that I was going to MAKE IT WORK.

Failure or going back to a job were no longer options.

Be Flexible

The great thing about how you'll make the leap using The Lifestyle Masterplan™ is that it is very flexible. You can always adjust or change course if it isn't working the way you want it to. *Never abandon course – adjust course.* Be willing to change course any time you need to. This book, in fact, is a considerable course adjustment from my original direction. That's not failure, that's success. Adjusting your course is part of being successful. Don't see your idea or concept as sacred or in cement, rather view it as flexible. This mindset will allow you to adapt to market changes and things you learn as they arise.

Be Committed

This mentality of "I will figure it out" is very freeing. I remember the night when I was sitting in bed frustrated because I could not figure out how I would ever make the leap from my full-time job and the salary that I so depended on to being an entrepreneur. As I was reading a business book, I made a monumental decision. I decided that I was going to figure out how to do it, how to make that leap, how to transition from working full-time to being an entrepreneur. I did not know *how*

> I made the decision "Tony-Robbins-style." As Tony puts it, "A real decision means cutting yourself off from any other possibility." It's important for you to decide that there is absolutely no other possibility than to succeed. It will happen. Period.
> howtoquitworkingbook.com/decisionmaking

I was going to figure it out, but I knew I *would* figure it out.

The idea of being willing to adjust your course requires a great deal of humbleness. It requires that you never get married to an idea or concept, and that you are willing and able to say to yourself, "Hmm, I thought that was going to work, but it didn't. Oh well...NEXT!"

Fire Your Ego

Don't let your ego get in the way of your success. If your ego is so strong that it won't let you change or admit you are wrong, you need to fire it. Fire your ego. It's not serving you; it's holding you back. How incredibly ironic is it that your ego's extremely strong desire for success is exactly the thing that is keeping you from being successful? Your desire to be right is the barrier between you and the course adjustments you need to make to be successful — so get rid of the ego.

Paycheck-To-Paycheck

A frightening proportion of people in this world live paycheck-to-paycheck, so if their paycheck is two days late, they are in a world of hurt. I remember living this way many years ago. Fortunately, I got away from this long before I left my corporate job. If this is currently your situation, you will need to fix that before you take a leap as an entrepreneur.

Try this exercise: Ask yourself what it would be like if you had no ego. I mean absolutely no ego whatsoever. If you think you don't have one, you are wrong. We all have some ego; it's just the way humans are.

If this is the case for you, you are dependent on that paycheck in a more serious way than others are. You are dependent on it to put the next meal on the table. I am not suggesting that you throw caution to the wind and use these techniques with the expectation that they will put a meal on the table in two weeks — because they won't.

Therefore, if you are in a paycheck-to-paycheck situation, you must fix that before you make the leap into entrepreneurship. This may not be as hard as you think. In all likelihood, it probably means being willing to give things up — give up the meals out, the expensive luxuries, etc.

I'm not here to teach you how to get your finances in order; however, I will recommend several resources that you'll find here:

howtoquitworkingbook.com/finances

You do need to have this in order before starting your entrepreneurial journey. I felt as though I needed six months of savings to make the leap; that is what made me comfortable. You will obviously need to decide what makes you comfortable.

The great thing about The Lifestyle Masterplan™ is that you can start working on it WHILE you are righting your financial ship.

You just have an additional item to check off your list. That's OK, after all you have committed to give things up, right?

OK, so go!

You Don't Have To Mortgage Your House And Wipe Out Your Savings

I can hear you saying this right now, "What are you talking about? You want me to quit my job, wipe out my savings and take a second mortgage on my house to start a business?"

No, that would be silly.

I'm here to show you another way. What if you could start slowly? What if you could start by doing something on the side? How would you like to get your business rolling and then expand it a bit? What if you began with a seedling of a business and a customer base (who are primed buyers) before you quit your full-time job? *That's* what The Lifestyle Masterplan™ is all about.

Since you've made the decision to be willing to give things up, you are ready to go. You are ready to start putting some time into this while you are still working.

One of the greatest things about building an expert lifestyle business is that, by its nature, it is flexible and can be done at any time of day and with a very small financial investment. The beauty of this is that you can get things rolling on the evenings and weekends while you are still working a full-time job, running your business, or whatever your primary income source is. Then, once you have laid your foundation and built a following, you are much closer to income, which is a great time to take the "leap!"

Taking Risks

I've thought long and hard about this. The ability to take risks is very important, and I understand why all the business leaders and entrepreneurs say "you have to take risks." The truth is though, once I got my mind right and made my solid commitments, I didn't feel like I was taking a risk. I DECIDED I was going to be successful. I made the decision that I was going to *make it work* somehow, some way. I committed that I wasn't going to stop until it worked.

Control & Sacrifice

Everything changes when you decide that you are not going to let anyone else have control of the situation. In other words, you are not going to blame clients, partners, market conditions, bad ideas, banks, competitors or ANYONE ELSE. Once you decide that you are in complete control, you are.

You also need to be willing to make sacrifices. Be willing to stay up late to get things done, to give up your weekends sometimes, and to give up indulgences because your limited funds are needed to invest in the business.

Keeping Control: If Billy didn't hold up his end of the bargain, don't BLAME Billy. That gives HIM the control. Figure out how YOU could change that next time. Maybe that means not working with Billy again. Perhaps it means making expectations clearer to Billy in the future. It doesn't matter; it only matters that YOU are deciding how YOU could have done it differently. Put the control back into YOUR hands.

Since you are in complete control and willing to make sacrifices, and now that your ego is no longer in charge, you are free to make whatever adjustments are necessary to be successful. If you see something not working, you can change it. You can adjust your course. You aren't wasting time and giving up control by blaming others, and you aren't afraid to make the sacrifices it takes to adjust course.

Finally, since you made your decision Tony-Robbins-style, you cut yourself off from any other possibility other than success. So how can you fail? You don't fail unless you quit; so if you never quit, you never fail. Problem solved!

Stop Worrying

Let's summarize how to stop worrying about this decision:

1. *Lose your ego.* If your ego is in check, you don't have the silliness of pride, or fear of being perceived as wrong or stupid, stopping you from making the course corrections that you will inevitably need to make.
2. *Be willing to give things up.* You have to be willing to make sacrifices and to do whatever it takes to be successful. Making these sacrifices is much easier when you keep in mind the awesome life you are creating. With your dream life in mind, those little things become much less important.
3. *Make your decision Tony-Robbins-style.* Make a real decision that means you cut yourself off from any other possibility. It is not an option to quit. You simply keep going until you are successful.
4. *Don't blame anyone.* Don't blame anyone for what happens — not even you. Look at what you need to do to make it different next time. If you blame someone else, you *give them the control*. You need full control in order to be successful, so don't do that to yourself.

If you can do these four things, you will have nothing to fear. All your fears can be answered by one or more of these four steps.

Unbelievable Opportunity

When in history have you EVER had access to as much information (i.e. the internet) right in the comfort of your home, or in the palm of your hand, as you do today?

NEVER.

There has never been as much information available and as many inexpensive resources for entrepreneurs as there are today. Period. It has never been so easy. I definitely could have built the business I built prior to the internet and social media, but there is no way I could have built it as quickly or as cheaply. This is an amazing opportunity you must take advantage of now!

Appreciate the world you are starting your business in. It is one of a huge amount of possibility and potential.

Conclusion

People will tell you that you are nuts. They are just trying to protect you, not realizing they are putting you in a cocoon and preventing you from being happy. Smile; thank them for their input; and keep doing what you are doing. They don't realize they are killing your dreams. Don't listen to them and don't hold it against them, they mean well.

You are creating something amazing and nobody can stop you. You are building a business structure that is going to make your life *exactly what you want it to be*. It will give you the freedom to spend your time *the way you want to* and doing the things that matter to you. Don't let fear or ego get in your way. This is too important.

Think Of It Like This:

- ✓ YOU are in charge. This is YOUR life.
- ✓ Every minute you spend worrying about the future, or regretting the past is a minute you could be spending shaping your life.
- ✓ The only decisions that really matter are made Tony-Robbins-style, meaning you cut yourself off from any other possibility.

Do It Like This:

- ✓ Fire your ego. If this is hard for you, just ask yourself once a day what your life would be like if you had no ego.
- ✓ Commit to giving things up or to making temporary sacrifices to create an amazing life for yourself.
- ✓ Take control of your success and decide to stop worrying.

Chapter 3

Make Thirteen Decisions

"It is in your moments of decision that your destiny is shaped."
- Tony Robbins

I've made several attempts at starting businesses, but I was never Ready. It took me a long time to get Ready. Along the way, I didn't know how to get Ready, or that I even was getting Ready. All I knew is that I kept putting one foot in front of the other as best I could.

In retrospect, I was forming the mindsets and making the decisions that would allow me to finally take the most difficult step of my journey — to quit my good-paying, secure, full-time corporate job and jump head-first into my business, and into a lifestyle of freedom.

As I explained previously, while I was trying to figure out the why and the how, I chose to leave the security of my corporate job and make the leap. As I reflected back, I saw thirteen key decisions that shaped who I've become and enabled me to make that big, scary leap.

What's interesting is that the thirteen things that most impacted my success were not things I was born with, given, or that I could even buy. They were DECISIONS — decisions that I consciously made and that allowed me to launch my dream life. Anyone who makes these thirteen decisions (and I mean MAKES the decisions) can literally do ANYTHING they want — they're that powerful!

Now I've engrained these so deeply in my life that I simply cannot imagine LIVING without these thirteen core values. The following list is the culmination of seventeen years of trying to figure out how the hell life works.

Thirteen Decisions That Will Change Your Life

Let's go.

1 - Decide To Be Honest.

For the most part, I think I've always been an honest person, but in my early twenties I decided to take this commitment to another level. I was going to be honest in a very big way — this meant not only telling the truth, but also being true to who I am and what my values are. It meant always doing what my values guided me to do.

When we don't act according to our values, we end up with regrets and things that haunt us. Some examples include:

cheating on your spouse/significant other, lying about something and it ends up causing harm, or not blowing the whistle in a situation (when you know you should but are afraid of the consequences). When I was not fully honest, I not only left a trail of regrets behind me, but I also discovered that I didn't like myself much. That's why I made it a personal policy that I will always do what I know is right.

Here's an example: Many years ago, a friend of mine left my apartment completely intoxicated. I believe he had finished a 750ml bottle of vodka. After I tried very hard to get him to stay at my apartment, he still insisted on leaving (and driving). This was one of the first times I took action based on my decision to tell the truth and follow my values. I remember thinking about it for only a short time and then decided to call the police. I got his license plate number and dialed 911.

My mindset was that I would rather damage our friendship (which was also my fear) than be someone who would allow something dangerous to occur. He made it home okay; the police did not catch up to him. However, the important thing was that I didn't have to wonder "What if?" — I had done what I knew I needed to do. While consistently making these types of decisions is not easy, it's a lot easier than living with yourself when you're not true to your values!

2 - Decide To Be Selfish.

Helping other people is one of the most rewarding things you can do in life. In fact, it is a large reason why I seek freedom — so I will have the ability to help others as I wish. But, you must help yourself first. You need to have your own house in order. Once you have done that, you are then able to help a great many more people, if that is what you desire.

I recognized that in order to be the best person I could be, both for me and for my friends and family, I had to put myself first. I had to BE who I was going to BE, in order to best serve those around me.

I believe the value of being selfless (always putting others first) is counterproductive and will not help me to become who I want to become. I will be able to do much more good when I am living as my best self. Not when I am living in servitude to everyone else at the expense of myself.

For example, if you spend all your time helping not-for-profits or those less fortunate, yet you neglect yourself by not pursuing your dreams, living by your values, and taking care of your needs, then you are failing to become that person who can do much more good and be even happier, and have an even greater influence on the world.

3 - Decide To Never Regret Anything. Ever.

I never regret anything. Period. I've never regretted a single thing in my life and I never intend to. I've had a long journey to get to where I am now, but the bottom line is this: everything I've done, right or wrong, good or bad, has contributed to who I am now and I'm quite happy to be in this place. So why should I regret anything?

Whatever I did or whatever happened is over. That's it. There is absolutely nothing I can do about what I did or didn't do in the past. Here is a really, really important point:

Every single second you spend regretting the past is a second you could spend shaping your future.

Once you let go of the past, you are paving your way to an awesome future; you are freeing up a tremendous amount of energy that will propel you forward to do amazing things.

4 - Decide To Listen.

When I began to listen more closely (really listen), I realized something very important: very seldom is anyone just plain wrong or lying.

What we perceive as incompetence, dishonesty or malicious intent rarely is. What happens is that people are viewing the situation from a different perspective than we are. They are seeing the situation through a lens that is completely different from our lens.

As you listen to someone, you can do one of two things. You can either slap a label of right or wrong, liar or honest, on them OR you can truly listen and understand their perspective and where they are coming from. What you will find when you listen closely is that you no longer learn simple facts; instead you begin to see a whole new perspective or viewpoint on the situation.

> It is very important to recognize that you have to be quiet in order to listen. This means your internal talk is quiet also. If you are thinking about what you're going to say next, then you are not being a good listener.

Small people view the world as right or wrong, black or white. Visionary people work to understand the various and diverse perspectives of others; and will become better human beings and more effective leaders as a result.

5 - Decide To Never Blame Anyone Or Anything.

This decision is of the utmost importance.

Never, ever blame anyone for anything ever, ever, ever. If you want to completely disempower yourself, blaming others is the fastest way to do it. When you blame others, you completely remove your ability to DO anything about the situation and leave yourself helpless and defeated; this also leaves the other person in charge of the situation.

Deciding that there is never anyone to blame is the only way to take charge of your life and get what you want. It is the ONLY way to actually TAKE control of your life. If you don't, it will always be someone else's fault; you will remain the victim and will not get what you want out of life.

When something doesn't go the way you wanted it to, you will decide which of these two questions to ask yourself:

    1.   Whose fault was it?
OR
    2.   What could I have done differently?

(Hint: the second question puts you in CONTROL of the situation.) Let's look at a situation where you were wronged by someone and let's see how these two questions can lead you in two different directions.

The first question gives you an answer that takes you nowhere. You might know that it was the other person's fault, but that doesn't help you or solve anything.

The second question gives you something that will allow you to act differently in the future, i.e. you might decide that you won't do business with that person again, or you might come up with a vastly different approach if you do need to work with them again.

6 - Decide To Set Goals.

Set goals — goals that you will miss, but will come close to achieving. Without goals, life is aimless wandering. That works for some people, but not for me. Once I decide I want something, I will do everything I can to get it.

Missing goals is not a bad thing. I think hitting goals is worse. What could you have done if you had just set your goal higher?

I have experimented a lot with this in my life. I have had goals, high and low, but generally I set them too high. While it is important to reach for the stars, it is just as important to have a mix of goals that are attainable and unattainable.

"The greatest danger for most of us is not that our aim is too high and we miss it, but that it is too low and we reach it." - Michelangelo

In other words, if they are too crazy high you will become frustrated and that doesn't help either.

The only way to figure this out (how high or low they should be) is with practice. Practice, practice, practice. Don't be afraid to fail. If you're afraid to fail, your goals will be painfully low and you won't grow, or you might become too fearful to set any.

7 - Decide To Be Positive.

Be positive. View every situation as an opportunity. What looks like a bad situation could very well turn out to be something wonderful — you just don't know yet. We frequently view loss, or perceived loss, as a bad thing. This perception is the root of much unhappiness in the world. What we often forget is that when things go away, space opens up for new things to enter. This can be very exciting!

Obviously there is not always something wonderful that is waiting on the other side of a bad situation (or one you've perceived as bad), but you still have a choice — you get to decide how you are going to deal with it. You always have the option to choose to maintain a positive attitude and figure out how you can learn from the situation and take something good from it.

This is a really hard one, particularly for me. The most important thing to do is to surround yourself with positive people who uplift you and create a happy, positive atmosphere in your world.

Sometimes that means you have to let go of the negative people. They can have a draining effect on your attitude, happiness, and on your ability to create, do or accomplish. This is not an easy step, but in the long run it is best for everyone.

8 - Decide To Be Yourself.

I realized at some point that people like me a lot more when I am myself, when I relax and say and do what comes naturally to me. Those are also the times when I like myself the most. The ironic thing is that generally when I've NOT been myself it has been because I was afraid of NOT being liked or accepted. And it ends up having the opposite effect! No one wants to be around a phony, and when you are phony, it shows.

Deciding to be yourself will require you to make another important decision. You need to decide that you DON'T CARE if people like you! This can be a hard decision (and quite a scary one) because we've been taught that being accepted is a significant part of our identity, and is important in our society.

While being myself results in more people liking me, there are and always will be some people who won't, and I'm OK with that. The most important thing to remember is that in all likelihood, no matter who you are, more people are going to dislike "the fake you" than will dislike "the real you."

9 - Decide To Clean Your Brain.

Turn off the TV — it's rotting your brain. Yes, the old saying is true! And the same goes for news media. Be careful about what you put into your brain. Why waste your valuable time sitting in front of that box? I got rid of all the TVs in my house. I will never live in another house with a TV.

I don't think there is anything wrong with TV in itself; I have a problem with a) the garbage that is on it and b) the RIDICULOUSLY EXCESSIVE amount of time the average person spends sitting in front of that box, just to be entertained.

The news is full of negativity; spending 30 minutes every day watching the "entertaining" horrors of the world (I'm referring to the six o'clock news) serves no purpose, except to put truckloads of negativity into your head and to drain you of time and energy.

I now consume exactly zero news. It's the best decision I ever made.

As far as entertainment television is concerned, I do have a few guilty pleasures which are mostly cartoon shows on the internet, but I limit myself to no more than a half hour a week (usually less). There, I admitted it publicly. Long, embarrassed sigh...

10 - Decide To Work On You.

You are your biggest and most important project. Constantly work on yourself and make yourself the best "YOU" you can be. Read, learn, get training, etc.

I read at least one book a month (non-fiction) and attend a lot of training (online, offline and in-person). I have also spent a considerable amount of money on myself. Again, that's money I spent on training, coaching, consulting, etc. There is no better investment than investing in your personal growth and development.

And, there comes a point when you have to DO. Keep a balance between learning and doing. There is such a thing as learning too much — that is when you are learning in lieu of doing. It's easy to become addicted to learning and to developing yourself, but at some point you have to stop learning and start DOING.

I have actually put myself on a "training diet" from time to time when I reached this point!

11 - Decide To Be Healthy.

Take care of your body. If your body is messed up or not in its best shape, your whole life will be too.

This is another one that I struggle with, but I believe it is very important and I've seen the benefits of doing it and the downside of not doing it. My body is the vehicle through which I do everything, so taking care of it obviously needs to be a priority.

Eat right; drink plenty of water; get exercise, and all that other good stuff. Why? I've found that when I take care of my body and care for myself, I feel more self-respect, am happier, more productive, and more fulfilled.

12 - Decide To Deliver On Commitments.

Do what you say you are going to do. More importantly, do what you DECIDE you are going to do. This is partially about appearances and gaining trustworthiness, but it is even more about learning to trust yourself.

I wish I could remember where, but I once read about creating a habit of failure. A habit of failure is when you fail to keep commitments so often that you subconsciously know that you will never (or rarely) keep a commitment. As a result, you make commitments randomly and arbitrarily without any intention of keeping them. I think that is a very, very dangerous road to start down.

I know that feeling of knowing deep down that you won't keep your commitments, so making them begins to feel meaningless. In the moment, it is the easiest thing to do, so you make commitments casually with no intention of keeping them.

The solution to this is to make fewer commitments. There is no sense in trying to make and keep a ridiculous number of commitments. Begin by making fewer of them, and keeping those. I now place myself under no obligation to MAKE commitments, but a strong obligation to KEEP commitments.

When you truly commit to keeping your commitments, you will find yourself thinking hard before you make a commitment. That is a good thing!

13 - Decide To Give Stuff Up.

I'm referring mainly to the categories of time and money. This was the final decision that allowed me to make my leap out of Corporate America. I decided that I would give up some of my comforts and short-term desires; I would give up some time with friends and family; I would give up eating out (that I so enjoyed); and I would give up the idea of being able to buy what I wanted when I wanted.

In other words, I chose to make sacrifices. What I now know is that they don't even seem like sacrifices when you are doing it for something you love and are following your dream. You only thought you needed them because you grew so accustomed to having them.

This is an incredibly important part of becoming an entrepreneur. You have to give stuff up — but you are doing so in exchange for much bigger things to come. So give it up with pleasure!

Conclusion

Thirteen decisions allowed me to pursue (and get) the life of my dreams! I did it and you can too. No one put this list in front of me when I was 22; I figured it out by living life and leaning into what I wanted.

If you want to launch your dream life of freedom, ask yourself this:

What is one small thing I can do today to get started?

It doesn't matter what it is or how small it is, just do it. Then do something else tomorrow. And the next day. And the next day. Until you have built the life of your dreams.

Think Of It Like This:

- ✗ You are in charge of your life and your destiny.
- ✗ You will be successful because you make a series of DECISIONS about how you approach life.

Do It Like This:

- ✓ Go through each of the thirteen decisions and DECIDE for yourself. What will you DECIDE to do and not do?
- ✓ Write down your decisions and keep the list in front of you.
- ✓ Look at your decision list daily and recommit to each decision.
- ✓ Take action on your decisions. Begin to make the changes you need to make to fully implement your decisions.

Chapter 4

Marketing in the 21st Century

""The aim of marketing is to know and understand the customer so well the product or service fits him and sells itself."
— Peter Drucker

Before we really dive into the meaty "how do you actually do this stuff" part of this book, we have to talk about marketing and how the heck it actually works in the 21st century.

But first, I have to bust a big myth.

The I-Myth

From here on, I'm going to call Internet Marketing 'Shminternet Shmarketing.' I'm so sick of hearing about it that I can't even stand to hear it said!

When I started building and promoting my business, I gravitated toward Shminternet Shmarketing. After all, I had managed website conversions for the largest financial institution mergers ever done in the US; and I had been a computer programmer for many years prior, so the Shminternet thing seemed like a logical fit.

All you have to do is put up a squeeze page, some videos, social media and BAM! You're in business!

Not exactly.

All my experiences in this area over the past several years resulted in me creating a term called the I-Myth. The I-Myth is the myth that it is actually POSSIBLE to build a real business by sitting behind your computer using squeeze pages, emails and social media.

And it is just that — A MYTH.

I'm not saying those things are bad or ineffective, but they are only tools. They are tools in your very large marketing toolbox. And they are only effective when used in conjunction with a real marketing strategy and plan.

Tactics Are Not Enough

What has happened in the past several years is that there has been a lot of internet momentum. Many things have changed resulting in lots of people having success using the internet as a marketing platform. Change always brings opportunity. This created a huge hunger for knowledge about marketing on the internet. Many of those successful people have packaged up what they did on the internet into products they portray as "complete marketing solutions" or even worse "complete business solutions."

But they are not COMPLETE marketing solutions, and they certainly are not complete BUSINESS solutions. They are a collection of tactics or techniques. Most of us have purchased these "complete marketing solutions" hoping they would give us the same results. We are usually disappointed.

That doesn't mean these packaged-up tactics are bad. They generally are good tactics, but they are just that — tactics. By themselves, they are not enough. They are only successful when executed as part of a complete and total strategy.

We give the internet too much credit. We say it has changed everything. And it has changed many things, but one thing it has not changed is the basic way that we market. Everything we do, even today, is based on basic and solid marketing principles that have been around for centuries. Yes, the way we deliver that marketing has changed, but the concepts have not. When we begin to view internet marketing as a concept that is NEW or that has CHANGED EVERYTHING, we neglect to adhere to the basics that are critical to successful marketing.

I will talk a lot in this chapter about how things have changed, but remember we are still working with basic marketing concepts that are centuries-old. Put that framework around everything you do.

Nobody Cares About You

I'm serious, nobody cares about you.

> They don't want to visit your website.
> They don't want to follow you on Twitter.
> They don't want to be your friend.
> They don't want to read your blog.
> They don't want to hear you speak.
> They don't want to buy your product.
> They don't want to receive your newsletter.

You cannot effectively become known for your knowledge if you don't accept this simple fact. You have to think like this in everything you do if you want to be successful in this industry. What this means is letting go of your ego. Your ego is telling you that people can't wait to follow you on Twitter, go to your website, hear you speak, read your book, etc. They can wait, and they will. Those are mediums of communication. Nobody cares about the medium; they want the benefit that comes from it. Most people would be perfectly happy if all those things went away!

Print out this list of statements (above) and put it in front of you while you are writing everything you write and doing everything you do, as you are getting known for your knowledge.

I've seen several horrible examples of this lately. In the past week, I've seen two people post, email or tweet something like: "Help me become an Amazon bestseller!" Why? I don't even know who the hell you are, much less what your book is about or why it will help me. "Get my book that will show you how to close more deals on the golf course" would be a much more effective way to approach this.

I know I'm being a downer, but it's for your own good. You have to realize it's not about you; it's about your prospect.

Now let's talk about what people DO want.

The Message Is King

There is good news — even though people don't care about you, they do care about your message. They want you to deliver value to them. They want to know what you can do for them. People are tuned into radio station WII FM (What's In It For Me). They are not tuned into WWSCIGTT (What Web Site Can I Go To Today). Nobody wants a website to go check out. They have plenty of other, more important things to do. They have enough websites to go to. You seriously can't LIVE in the civilized world for more than five minutes without somebody trying to get you to go to their damn website! In all likelihood, the website is total crap and is trying to sell me some garbage that I don't want or need. And that is exactly what people are thinking, no matter what, when they hear you talk.

If you seriously want me to have an aneurysm, tell me to "go check out" your website.

> By the way, if you are bored, go check out my website at www.nobodygivesacrap.com.

Your message is not about the medium; it's about the benefit. Your message should be "Learn the 13 Decisions that Allowed me to Launch my Dream Life," not "Go check out my website for lots of great stuff." Lots of great stuff? What? When someone reads that, they think, "What the hell is he trying to sell me?"

"Go check out my website" worked great in 1996. People had just started surfing the internet and were DYING to play with it; they were looking for new websites to go to!

"I think I'm going to get on the internet today," we would say. "Hmm, what websites can I go to?"

In 1996, if someone said, "Go check out my website," we said, "Yay — a website! I'm going to go check it out. Hey guys, look it's one of those new WEBSITE thingies!"

You Are Expected To Have A Website

But as more and more people and businesses began publishing on the internet, it soon became a natural assumption that if you were anybody, you or your business would have a website. The mentality shifted from:

"Wow, you have a website? That's awesome."

to

"What? You don't have a website?"

Then along came blogs and free websites. Suddenly EVERYONE could get their message out there quickly, easily and cheaply. We had critical mass (by critical mass, I mean we had a ton of awful websites with lousy content) on the internet. Most people were on the internet and there was a lot of momentum. It was going crazy.

Then came Web 2.0, as social media entered the picture. That is really the point at which the noise on the internet became so deafening that nobody could hear a damn thing.

Why is this history of the internet important? Because it guides how we market today.

Provide Value

Here is what you always have to keep in mind —be CONSISTENTLY CONSCIOUS of the fact that there are BAZILLIONS of people also trying to get a message out there. In order to be successful, you have to stand out in that very crowded environment. You have to be different.

I'm not talking about having a bunch of silly gimmicks or catch phrases, or even having a crazy personality. While those approaches can be very effective (the crazy, eccentric and opinionated personality is working very well for me), first and foremost, you have to provide VALUE. You have to provide value that is better than AND unique from everyone else out there. That is how you get noticed today.

When I say unique, I really mean unique. And that shouldn't be hard. When you decided to get known for your knowledge, I doubt you said, "I want to repeat the same crap that everyone else has been saying for years, exactly how they've been saying it." No! You wanted to offer people something different — you have something UNIQUE to say. In fact, you are probably tired of hearing what everyone has to say, tired of the spin they put on it, tired of the main points they make, and tired of the way they deliver their message. You wouldn't be passionate about it if there were tons of people saying the exact same thing that you want to say!

I think I have sufficiently broken you down; I've destroyed your self-confidence, broken your spirit and you might even be crying.

It's going to get better. Keep reading.

The Biggest Mistake

Here's the great news: If you do everything you do with the notion that nobody cares about you, you will have great success. The biggest mistake people make in this industry is to assume that people automatically want their stuff. They don't. People want help; they want solutions; they want hope. Give them that. You have it — you just need to COMMUNICATE it.

Every time you communicate with your followers, communicate what you have to offer — this doesn't mean your "offer" of a six-disk CD set! It means you communicate that you offer a better way to run their popsicle stand that will increase their profits and give them more free time to spend with their family. Communicate that you can teach them a technique to meditate for only five minutes a day so they can live a happier, more fulfilled life. Or you can try asking them to check out your web site — you'll see the difference for yourself.

On your way to getting known for your knowledge, one of the things you'll learn through The Lifestyle Masterplan™ is how to clearly define your VALUE. You will define what makes you different than anyone else who does something similar. You'll write out WHAT you have to offer, WHO you offer it to, and most importantly, WHY they want it.

Talk Like A Person

> 'At Braveau Experts, we believe it is very important to communicate in a manner that is extremely professional and polished. It is a key differentiator to ensure that all your

> *communication mediums consistently represent
> Braveau Experts' corporate brand. Numerous
> studies have shown that a consistent strategic
> brand positioning strategy will propel the brand
> to strongly-differentiated success.'*

What the hell?

That's talking like a corporation. Don't do that, it sounds so dumb. Talk like a person. Chill. (I grew up in the 80's when we said, "chill out." Chill sounds less dorky so that's why I say it.) Be you. Talk like you normally talk. Write the way you talk.

As a personal example, I am a very strange, eccentric person. I'm completely nuts actually. I'm wound tighter than an 8-day clock. I cuss sometimes and use really off-the-wall analogies. And I can be dense at times. I'm the most introverted extrovert you will ever meet. Most of all, I am as GOOFY as they come. I'm the biggest goofball I know. I love to dance and sing, yet am terrible at both. And I love attention. So what?

I let all that come through in everything I do for my business. It is what makes me ME. It's why people remember me and like me. What? Just being my goofy, nutty self? Yes, that's exactly what does it. Just acting like a complete fool and saying exactly what pops into my head. I did tell you this is an amazing lifestyle, didn't I?

Be Who You Are

The hard part is to get comfortable with it. As kids, we were innocent, free, fearless and most importantly, exactly who we wanted to be! Then came the layers and layers of crap that our society put on top of us, telling us who to be, how to act and what to think. We then believe that we have to "be something" in order to be liked or known. And that simply isn't true. We just have to be who we naturally are.

This is hard. It really is. And the only thing I can tell you is to practice, because it gets a bit easier each and every time. Each time you write something, shoot a video, or whatever you do, be a little more "your-damn-self." Just let a little more of your-damn-self come out each time. Every time you do something, come out of your comfort zone a bit more. It will get easier and easier each time. Before you know it, you will be doing it without knowing it. You will be completely relaxed and won't even have to fake being real anymore.

Jeff sometime in the 80's

This is one that I struggle with — it really scares me! But it scares me less each time I do it. It scares me to write in this book that I'm scared; but I'm doing it anyway because I know that if I admit I'm scared, you will feel more connected with me and take me more seriously. Why? Because you are probably scared when you think about all this. Believe me, I understand that. And I know that what I'm doing is the right thing, and by being in touch with and open about who I am, I will be fine.

It's Okay To Stand Out.

I was NOT the popular kid. I was the dorky kid with giant glasses and a white kid's version of an afro; I liked to dress differently than the rest of the kids and had the hand-eye coordination of a donut. When we played dodge ball in PE, the other kids would make it a game to see who could hit Steinmann square in the face so his glasses would go flying across the gym. Which actually was pretty easy to do — it's not like there was a snowball's chance in hell that I was going to get out of the way fast enough! All this to say that I know all about not fitting in. I know what it's like to be laughed at and ostracized. If you are worried about that, I'm telling you right now, "Get over it."

You are an adult, not a 12 year-old in gym class. You have a life to live, and it's time to live it. Are you going to let the bullies of the world stop you? For me, it was bullies in gym class; for you, it's something else. The way I look at it is that I have two choices:

1. I can let those 12-year-old idiots (most of whom are now stuck in 9-5 jobs they hate) control what I do with my life.

OR

2. I can control what I do with my life.

I've made my decision.

Make Your Decision

For you, it's probably not 12-year-old bullies; instead it might be your boss, your sibling, your best friend, spouse or coworkers. But there is someone whose opinion you fear. There is someone you picture laughing at you when you think about opening up. Ask yourself this, "Who is going to win? Will it be me or will it be them?" Make a decision. Who is going to win?

There are two facts you must accept in order to fully embrace being who you are:

1. People will like you more if you'll 'be your-damn-self,' and
2. Some people won't like you if 'be your-damn-self.'

We are in the 21st century and everyone is tired of corporate, polished, high-level "we" talk. Everyone is simply fed up with it. They want REAL PEOPLE, REAL CONNECTIONS, and REAL RELATIONSHIPS.

The Corner Butcher

I was born too late. I probably should have been born around the turn of the century. Back in those days we didn't buy our meat at Wal-Mart; we bought it from Al. Al was the local town butcher who we knew, trusted and liked. We bought our meat from Al. Not from Al's Butcher Shop. We knew Al; we trusted Al; we cared about Al; and Al cared about us.

> *"Hi Al, I'm having company on Friday and need four of your best pork chops. How's your mom? I saw your sister at the park yesterday,"* we'd say to Al.

> *"I just got some great cuts from my best supplier. Let me wrap those up for you. Mom is doing well; she's slowing down, but hanging in there. We're going to have her and dad over for dinner on Saturday. Nothing perks her up like seeing her grandkids!"* Al replies.

Today we go to the meat counter and are greeted with a number dispenser. We take a number to mark our place in line. There's no butcher. Instead there is someone making minimum wage who wants nothing more than to slap some cold cuts into white paper, print off a sticker, and get us out of there, because they want to Tweet someone.

Be Your-Damn-Self

Humans crave that interaction with Al the butcher. We want a relationship with the people we do business with. If you are wondering how to compete with all the large players in your area of expertise, and there are likely several, just be your-damn-self! You will blow away the big, corporate players. Easily. Why? It's simple — they can't be themselves because they aren't people; they are large, faceless, legal entities. I'm not saying that's bad, but it does give you the distinct advantage of being able to be your-damn-self.

And remember that not everyone will like your-damn-self. So be OK with that. It is totally fine for people to not like you. If you get your mind right on the subject, you can actually enjoy and exploit your haters (but that's another book)! If you think, even for one moment, that everyone loves you, you are on crack. Seriously. There will be lots of people who won't like you.

Congratulations — Someone Didn't Like You

I have a close and trusted mentor who has helped me realize something very important about what I'm doing: if SOME people don't dislike me or disagree with what I'm saying, I'm not creating a true brand. When I see that I'm alienating some people, it's validation that I'm on the right track and that I'm creating a unique offering. (Of course it won't be right for everyone. It doesn't need to be. I only need it to be right for my niche.)

When I was working in the corporate world, whenever I spoke with someone who was feeling upset or down because they had made someone else mad or because someone didn't like what they were saying (particularly other project managers), I would reply, "If you aren't pissing somebody off, you probably aren't doing your job very well." And I strongly believe that.

This is also true when you are getting known for your knowledge. If you don't say or do anything that someone disagrees with or gets downright angry about, then you aren't saying anything meaningful. In fact, you don't have much of a message — you aren't saying anything new or different! That is what being an thought leader is about. It's going to piss people off; it's going to offend people; it's going to alienate people. That's OK.

It is totally OK if people don't like you. Accept it and be OK with it.

Be Vulnerable

You are not perfect. Thank goodness. That's a good thing. You have a story of struggle and humility that makes you unique, likeable and approachable. Run with it. LOVE IT! It's going to serve you well.

Is this going counter to the whole "nobody cares about you" thing I just talked about? No. Let's discuss why not. I said nobody cares about you and they don't. I also said that they DO care about what you can offer them (since I destroyed you earlier, now I'll build you back up).

Provide Value In A Unique Way

When you offer VALUE to customers IN A MANNER that is unique, memorable, sincere and genuine (in other words, when you are vulnerable and honestly share yourself and what you know), prospects will be hooked! They hear plenty of polished, corporate messages every day. Hearing from a real person who is relaxed and being him/herself is a breath of fresh air. And, more importantly, since it is genuine and sincere, they will believe it, and trust and like you even more.

How does this tie into the whole 'marketing in the 21st century' thing? THAT is how you will be heard. When you provide value in a genuine, sincere and memorable way, you will stand out far beyond anyone else with a similar message. And you will certainly stand out more than the others who are offering the 'same-old' tired messages. As you'll recall, it is soooo easy to get your message out to loads and loads of people, but that is completely useless if nobody hears it. In order to be heard, you have to provide value in a unique way.

Target Your Niche

Now that you've accepted the fact that not everyone is going to like you, let's talk about the group of people who ARE going to like you. These are the people with whom your ideas resonate; they feel a connection to you; they like you; they actually look at the stuff you

In architecture, a niche is defined as "a shallow recess, especially one in a wall, to display a statue or other ornament." And that is exactly what your niche is as it relates to the general population; it is a shallow recess of the general population.

publish; and most importantly, they want to buy your unique offering!

Now it's time for a harsh wake-up call. This group of people is not EVERYBODY. It's not even MOST PEOPLE. It is called your niche because it is a group of people who want what you offer.

To start, you will select a small, well-defined niche of people with considerably-similar attributes. You cannot target EVERYBODY. When I ask my clients, "Who can benefit from your knowledge?", invariably they reply with some version of "everyone." Their product/service/knowledge is so versatile that it can help anyone! They excitedly explain how everyone needs this product or service, and that even if they don't, they probably know someone who does; therefore, EVERYONE is their target demographic.

THIS DRIVES ME INSANE.

Your Niche Is Not "EVERYONE"

It drives me insane because the reason they say this is because they want to sell a lot of stuff. That mentality is a 100% guarantee that they will sell very little stuff. Nobody, and I mean nobody, can create a product that EVERYBODY wants. Not even Coca-Cola. I think Coke tastes awful. I also don't particularly care for Budweiser products, and I think the Snuggie is the dumbest thing ever invented. Those brands are intended to have very wide appeal. And they do. They also have massive marketing budgets. I'm guessing that you don't have a Coca-Cola-sized marketing budget.

So that means you have to narrow your niche to a manageable size that you can reach with the resources that you have.

Let's say you own a winery. You have a new wine coming out and you need a label for it. You start approaching graphic designers to design your wine label. You hear two distinctly separate messages:

1. "I can create graphics for anything! I have done billboards, TV graphics, post cards, web design, you name it!" (I love how enthusiastically this awful marketing message is typically delivered.)

2. "I specialize in graphic design for wineries. I can create a label and I've also created table cards for tastings and information sheets for many of my clients who own wineries."

Who are you gonna pick? It's pretty obvious, isn't it?

Niche-Down

You can't be scared to "niche-down." In the example above, the first designer has no way of differentiating him/herself among the large number of other graphic designers. That means they get lumped into the pot along with the McDonalds, Starbucks, and Coca-Colas of the graphic design world. They are now in a pot and competing with other companies/designers that they cannot afford to out-advertise.

Those big companies have the marketing budgets to make people think they need their products. McDonalds has actually convinced us that we LIKE that crap they are serving! These large companies still have a niche — it's just a very large one and they have the marketing muscle to appeal to that large group of people.

People getting into this business frequently are afraid that they are limiting themselves by getting more specific with their niche; and while that is somewhat true, it also positions you for success that you *can't achieve otherwise*. Further, once you have that success within your smaller niche, you can then transfer that success and momentum to other strategically-identified (and larger) niches.

Let me elaborate on that a bit. When you gain footing in a niche, it gives you momentum, followers and money that you can use to take your message further. The best way to get bigger is to get smaller. By successfully conquering a smaller niche, you gain the following, credibility and money you need to go after and market to larger niches.

So don't be afraid to get specific with your niche. Your success *depends on it*. Think of it as getting a foothold or as a necessary baby step before you build something bigger.

Build Relationships

I can summarize relationship-building in one word:

HUSTLE.

The first step is about plain, old-fashioned hustle. It's work! But it's fun work, and it's work that will pay you handsomely. But you will have to get your bootie out there and do it. Get out there and talk to people. Get out there and speak. Get out there and post valuable stuff on social media.

Social media is only ONE piece of the puzzle, not the cure-all, panacea that will change your life forever. You'll notice that I talk (read: rant) about this throughout the whole book.

Hustle

There are lots of great ways to build relationships and we'll talk more specifically about them in the chapter seven, but I want to talk more conceptually right now.

Building relationships means doing things for people for free; having lunch with contacts; randomly helping people you don't know and not charging them. Speak to groups of people for free. Put great content up on the internet through blogs, webinars and social media. Talk to people on social media. Attend networking events, and on and on and on. The point is that you are getting in front of as many people as you can with your message!

There Is No Magic Bullet!

The most important thing to remember here is that that this is simply hustling — getting out there and meeting people and building connections. This is where I struggled the most; partially because I was trying to build relationships and do much of this while I was still working full-time, but mostly because I was looking for the silver bullet. I was looking for the one magic thing that I could buy or do quickly that would get me a bunch of followers. I searched for that one thing for about three years and never found it. All I found were tactics, hype and gimmicks.

There are plenty of great and very effective techniques out there that you can buy or pay to learn about, or just learn about for free. But what they all come down to is hustle.

It doesn't matter how you promote. Forget "webinars are HOT right now!" Forget "Twitter is the best way to get leads!" Forget "speaking is the best way to get followers." Those are all great methods to build followers, but the simple fact is that it all comes down to hustle.

How Do You Get Their Attention?

How do you go about getting in front of people? How do you get your word out there? I'm going to warn you, this section is going to leave you with more questions than answers. It might even frustrate you if you are a real nuts-and-bolts kind of person.

Don't worry, though — I'll clear it all up in the next few chapters. I put this chapter right where it is so you wouldn't be confused for long. We will dive into the HOW in the very next chapter, so relax. It is important for you to understand this conceptually or the rest won't make a bit of sense. So stay with me.

Ready? Good, I knew you were.

Three Steps To Building An Expert Lifestyle Business

There are three main parts to building an expert lifestyle business in the 21st century:

1. Provide FREE and low-cost value to your prospects as an incentive to get them hooked.
2. Build relationships with them via blogging, speaking, writing, networking, webinars, social media, etc.
3. Sell your products and services to those followers.

That's all you have to do. You could probably stop reading right now. But I wouldn't recommend that because there's some really good stuff coming up!

Provide Valuable Free And Low-Cost Content

Create amazing content and promote it. Writing this book is the perfect example of this. This book is the most amazing, epic piece of content I have created to-date. After it is done, I'm going to promote it like you wouldn't believe. I'll be speaking about it, posting on Facebook about it, Tweeting about it, networking about it, going to events to talk about it, going on TV to promote it. You name it. I will be all over the damn place. And I will build a massive group of followers around it. That's all there is to it. Is it easy? Nope — it takes work and hustle. But it's fun.

Nobody wants me to tell you this part — this is just a lot of damn hard work. Most people don't want me to tell you that because they want to sell you their hyped-up product that promises you the sun, moon and stars for only two grand.

"How to get 700 Facebook fans every time you pee."

"How I built a six-figure business by Tweeting dictionary words."

"Six figures in six minutes by 'Pinning'."

You guessed it — I bought all those products. And don't get me wrong, there is some great stuff out there; but it's a combination of the way they are marketed and the way our brains are wired that causes us to seek instant gratification. This search for the magic bullet takes us to a place in our head that makes us say, "This is going to solve all my problems. This is the thing I've needed all along. It's my marketing messiah."

It's an oasis. There is no marketing messiah.

There are some great techniques in those $97.00 training programs. But I'll guarantee you they won't work if you don't hustle, and they won't work if they aren't part of a comprehensive, strategic business and marketing plan. Good thing you're reading this book!

Promote Your Content

Find great ways to promote it! I'll give you some techniques for promoting your content, and there are lots of methods out there that you can learn about. If you see some marketing product or program that speaks to you and you really want to try it, by all means, give it a shot. In all likelihood, there is something of value that you can get from it. As long as you recognize that it won't solve all your problems; it won't take away the work you have to do; and it won't be a silver bullet. Hustle will still be required. You still have to create great content and promote it.

Capture The Lead

Once you create your great content and have promoted it, you will then want to "capture the lead." In other words, get the prospects into your NET! You want a way to contact them again. You will be contacting them directly to provide more great content, but MOST IMPORTANTLY, to SELL to them! That is the final step in the lead generation / capture process: get their permission to contact them via email. Then you are in.

Permission To Email

The next step is to create products and sell them to the prospects on your list. I want to be clear that everything you have done up to this point was for the specific goal of getting the prospects' email addresses onto your list. That is your goal.

You don't want Facebook fans; you don't want Linkedin connections; you don't want attendees at your speech — the reason you do these things is to build the relationships so you can get the prospects' names on your email list. That is how you get permission to sell to your prospects. We'll talk a lot more about that in chapter seven, but for now, know that your main goal is to get "permission to email."

Conclusion

This chapter contained the main concepts that you will want to keep in mind as you build your expert lifestyle business. We'll get into more specifics of The Lifestyle Masterplan™ just as soon as you turn the page. You were smart to read this chapter thoroughly — it contains some of the most important concepts you'll need to build your expert lifestyle business.

Think Of It Like This:

- ✘ This takes work, there are shortcuts and some things are more effective than others, but there is no 'magic bullet' solution
- ✘ Marketing your expert lifestyle business is just providing valuable content in a unique and memorable way.

Do It Like This:

- ✓ Don't be afraid to get specific with your niche. It's what will bring you success.
- ✓ Deliver your message and value in a genuine, unique and memorable way. This is easy; just be your-damn-self!
- ✓ Don't fall for hype — you still have to hustle!

Chapter 5

Create Your Blueprint

"You can't plow a field simply by turning it over in your mind."
— Gordon B. Hinckley

When architects create blueprints, they don't make arbitrary decisions about things such as what type of concrete to use, how strong the steel should be, or how much support is needed. They make these decisions based on their education and experience as an architect, coupled with their knowledge of building codes, and through the application of proven mathematical calculations.

We are going to build a huge skyscraper, but first decide what you want to build. Just like an architect, before you can begin to create your blueprints you must know what you are building. Since we are talking about creating a LIFE that you love with all the freedom you want, the first thing you'll need to figure out is what you want your life to look like.

The first drawing that an architect does is called an elevation view. The elevation view is very simple. It's a drawing of what the building is going to look like from the outside when it's done. It doesn't have any structural specifications; it doesn't specify building materials; it doesn't have load calculations. It just shows what the building is to look like.

That's the first step in creating your blueprint — write down what you want your life to look like. Download the Lifestyle Elevation View at howtoquitworkingbook.com/elevationview, fill it out and pin it up where you will see it all the time.

Don't Repeat My Mistakes

I talked about my big mistake in chapter one. Remember when the coffee cup was shattered in the driveway? I had built a company that was completely incompatible with what I wanted my life to be like — that sudden realization awakened me.

I don't want you to have to admit to some silliness like that in your book, so let's get it right from the start.

After that pivotal awareness and the traumatic death of my beloved coffee cup, I got rid of all my clients and completely restructured my business. Starting from scratch in many ways, I created the Elevation View Worksheet so that I would never forget EXACTLY what I want my life to look like and so that I can make sure my clients also know exactly what they want their lives to look like.

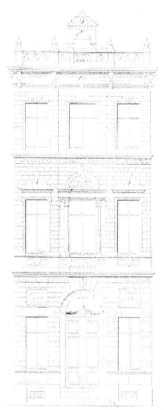

Front Elevation of the Museum Fodor in Amsterdam

Map Out Your Ideal Life

The Elevation View Worksheet asks you questions about who you are and helps you to get clear on what you want your life to be. Had I drawn my elevation view before launching my business, I would have gone in a different (and more congruent) direction with my company and avoided a lot of wasted time and effort.

If you haven't already created your Lifestyle Elevation View (in other words, you [foolishly] :) ignored my instructions in chapter one), then set this book down now and create it. If I'm giving you another opportunity to do this, you can assume (correctly) that it's THAT important!

howtoquitworkingbook.com/ elevationview

Now let's dive a little deeper. The next thing that architects do is to create the detailed architectural and structural views of the building. They draw out HOW the building will be constructed so that the elevation views will become reality. These are called plan views. That's what we're going to do next. We're going to draw out HOW you are going to create your expert lifestyle business.

The Knowledge View

The first "view" you will create is the Knowledge View. The Knowledge View outlines who you are, what you know, and why you do what you do. This is fundamental. You and your expertise are the centerpiece of your business and it's critical that you get really clear on this.

Who Are You?

Write a little bit about yourself. What's your background? What is your story? How did you get involved with your area of expertise? What do you like to do? It's OK to get personal on this. It's just for you at this point and sometimes inserting personal stuff is very powerful. You and your story will become the centerpiece of your expert lifestyle business, so take some time to get this right. It's important.

What Do You Know?

Clearly you have knowledge. You set out to launch an expert lifestyle business because you have something that you want to share. Is that a new method of breast feeding? Is it a more effective way to communicate with your teenagers? Is it a method of speech therapy that helps caregivers to teach people with severe speech problems how to talk? Is it a way to escape your 9-5 job? Whatever it is, write it down; spell it out. You don't have to put it down in excruciating detail, just write what comes naturally — relax and let the pen tell the paper what you offer.

How Did You Get That Knowledge?

Very few people (actually none) pop out of the womb as experts on anything, so tell us how you learned what you know. What did you learn, experience, do, try, not do, give up or whatever...to gain this knowledge? Were you suffering from severe allergies and decided to give an all-natural diet a try? Were you struggling to find a job and suddenly discovered a resume format that works better than all the others? How did you get to the point where you are now? Relax and be honest. This is just for you.

These stories are usually NOT pretty! You definitely experienced some struggle on your journey, right? If you think your story is: "I wanted to learn x so I learned x," you are probably not telling the whole truth. There was probably (most definitely) some struggle involved in getting to that place. Share your struggle — it helps people relate to you.

If you are worried that it might be damaging to admit to your struggle, consider this: You heard mine! It's in the Introduction. Did my story of struggle scare you? Did it make you think less of me? Did it make you stop reading? Nope. You kept reading. The fact that I shared my story may even be the reason you continued to read beyond the Introduction.

I'm also certain that however you found out about this book probably has something to do with my story, because I tell it every chance I get, so you may have heard it before. And you're still here, so I'm going to keep telling it.

Why Do You Do What You Do?

Your story usually flows nicely into your purpose. Why on earth is it *this*? Is it because you want to help other nursing mothers? Do you want to help other struggling young professionals make it big in the corporate world? Talk about why you have to share THIS message more than anything else.

You are an expert in something and the fact of the matter is, since you came out of the womb knowing ABSOLUTELY NOTHING, you could have become an expert on practically anything. Right? So why this particular subject? Why this instead of underwater basket-weaving? Your followers need to know WHY you are saying what you are saying and doing what you are doing.

I spent a lot of time (and money) with a consultant to get completely clear on my WHY. It was some of the best time and money I've ever spent.

My Why: After a 15-year career, the last part of which was completely unfulfilling and downright depressing for me, I left to pursue my dream of being an entrepreneur and owning a business. As I was getting my business off the ground, I found that I had an immense amount of passion for helping other people. I want to help people who feel stuck in a lifestyle that isn't working for them to find their freedom and live their dream life.

The utterly amazing thing is that I had already developed the business model — it was all there! I had this huge realization of WHY I had been doing all that I was doing. I realized that I want to help other people who are stuck in a job, business or other situation that is not giving them the freedom they want and NEED to be happy.

Why knowing your why is critical

I did it backwards — I created a business and then backed into my why. It worked out for me in the end, but did require a lot of backing up and restarting. I created The Lifestyle Masterplan™ so you don't have to make the same mistake I made. Get clear on this NOW, not after you've created the wrong kind of business.

It's really simple. If you are going to speak to your followers in a way that resonates with them and makes them want to listen to you, know you, love you, and most importantly, buy from you, then you must first have a solid grip on why the hell you are doing this!

If you don't think that knowing your WHY is important, watch this video:

howtoquitworkingbook.com/why

The Improvement View

There is absolutely no point in doing what you are doing unless it can actually IMPROVE people's lives. I really don't care for the word "expert" because it's too focused on what YOU KNOW. This isn't about what you KNOW, it's about what you IMPROVE. Think of everything you do with regard to how you can improve other people's lives. It's not that you have to totally transform someone's life in every way possible or in some drastic way. It can be as little as helping them build better model airplanes, but it must offer some way of making their lives a better, more enjoyable experience, no matter how large or small that change is.

How Do You Improve Lives?

Understand exactly what a listener, reader, follower, etc. will get from what you have to teach them.

How will their life be different after consuming your information?

You don't want to get deeply into the medium or method of delivery here. This isn't about saying, "I have a six-part CD series that will give you three new lovemaking techniques." This is about the transformation you are offering, not the means by which you are going to deliver it.

The most important part of this section is the benefit. What does your client or customer ACTUALLY GET? Again I'm not talking about CDs, books, training videos, etc.; I'm talking about the actual benefit. Do they get a better love life, a deeper connection with their children, more clients, a more rewarding and fulfilling career, or a happier, calmer life? Focus on benefits here, not means of delivery.

How Do You Create That Improvement?

This is where we start to discuss the HOW. But, we're still not talking about delivery means. We're talking about the process you take people through to create that transformation. Here's a hint, you are reading about mine!

What is it that you want people to do, not do, stop doing, start doing, do more of, do less of, do differently, or think differently about in order to create the improvement we just talked about?

Embedded in your knowledge is some action your clients need to take in order to get the improvement you are offering. If you could tell someone who needs your knowledge exactly what to do and in what order to do it, what would you tell them? The answer here cannot be:

1. Hire me as your coach,
2. Buy my product, or

3. Come to my event.

We are talking about something less specific. If you are a golf swing expert, you might have three main things that you teach students to focus on, such as Form, Focus and Power, or something like that. Think about the common elements or the common things you work with people on to improve their lives.

Perhaps you teach your clients to focus on a different aspect of their situation than is traditional. Maybe you teach them to view their situation differently? Or you may give them a new way of approaching it. What is it that you have clients DO that creates the improvement?

How Do You Do That Differently?

This is critical these days. There are probably many people who do what you do and you cannot be just like them. If you are just like them, you have no choice but to compete with them on price, i.e. be cheaper. That's no way to create a lifestyle.

You are a unique person (that's why we talked about your story and your "why" in the previous section). Because of that, you not only have a unique perspective but also a unique way of creating that improvement for your clients.

If you can't come up with something here, think harder. If you think there is nothing different about you and how you do what you do, you probably aren't giving yourself enough credit. Open your mind and consider everything about yourself that makes you unique. Then come up with a starting point.

This doesn't have to be perfect now and you may have to dive into your business before you really understand this at the level you need to. That's OK, because The Lifestyle Masterplan™ is designed to give you information about your niche all along, so you're on the right path. Just get started.

What Are The Common Steps?

When you create this improvement for your clients, there will be some common set of steps you take them through. For example, I have a three-part system for creating an expert lifestyle business:

1. Cement Your Foundation,
2. Erect Your Structure, and
3. Raise Your Spire.

It's called The Lifestyle Masterplan™ and you're reading about it now. You must also break what you do down into a system — this gives you a simple, easy way to talk about what you do.

Think about a fun and interesting way to organize and present the information. Generally you should have three to seven steps to the system. Fewer than three isn't a process, and more than seven is overwhelming. Consider using a backronym, which is where you pick a word and then create steps to turn that into an acronym. For example, the last step of my process uses a backronym of "SPIRE."

> **S**urvey your followers
>
> **P**ractice teaching in an interactive situation
>
> **I**ntegrate what you know into a hands-off product
>
> **R**efine that product
>
> **E**xpand your reach with JV partners

We'll talk more about this in chapter eight.

Relax On This One

Don't stress about this. You DO have to start thinking about it now, but it doesn't have to be perfect yet. It takes time to get clear on this, so just do the best you can; the method you use to improve lives will change and evolve over time, so just get a starting point in mind now.

The Niche View

Just as you defined WHO you are and WHAT you offer as an expert, now you need to get clear on WHO you offer it to. You may have guessed that this means answering four questions:

1. Who are they?
2. What are their problems and aspirations?
3. What is their view of the world?
4. Where can you find them?

Who Is Your Niche?

This one is REALLY, REALLY, REALLY important.

This is how most people think about their niche:

> *"I am going to target the largest group possible. The more people I can target, the more sales I will make!"*

Wrong!

Here is another popular misconception:

> *"I can teach you how to start a successful lawn-care business. Everyone should want this product! I'm certain a lot of young men will like this product because it will teach them how to make money with a skill they already have, and it requires no experience or education, but others will want it too. Even if someone can afford to have their lawn mowed, they might want another source of income. Who wouldn't want to start a lawn-care business?"*

But this logic is simply not valid. Why? Because…

THERE ARE A LOT OF PEOPLE WHO DON'T WANT TO START A LAWN-CARE BUSINESS!

Using this example, the target audience needs to be niched down to males between 16 and 22, who have $500 to invest in a new business, and who want to earn money to save up for a big purchase (probably a car). Think about the powerful, benefits-driven message you can write to THAT specific niche (versus trying to market to everyone)!

> *"I can teach you how to make enough money to have the down payment for a car and three months of insurance money IN THE BANK in just ONE summer by starting your own lawn-care business. You'll be picking up girls in your car by the time school starts."*

There we go! That's what niching does for you.

Niche Down To Be Successful

You need a narrow-enough niche so that you can write to them that specifically and in that compelling of a manner. Don't be greedy with niche definition. It doesn't serve you. At all. As you saw in this simple example, the greedier you are with your niche selection, the less success you will have.

> WARNING: I'm going to get on a soapbox now because this is something that drives me insane. If I had a nickel for every time I had this conversation with a client, I'd have a BIG jar of nickels! This ties in with my previous explanation of the humbleness that is required in this industry.

You (probably) don't have the marketing budget of Coca Cola, Anheuser Busch or McDonalds. Those are products that appeal or at least attempt to appeal to EVERONE. Almost everyone is their potential customer. Despite that, Coke, Budweiser and the McDouble are not GREAT products; they are mediocre products (at best) that have been brilliantly branded and marketed. These brands have been built over many, many years by some of the best advertising agencies (not by a single person and a couple of contractors). These companies have the advertising power to actually MAKE you want something that you may or may not otherwise have wanted.

In Architecture, a niche is defined as a shallow carve-out of a larger structure, usually for holding statuary. Just like your niche is a carve-out of the general population. Image courtesy of "Ji-Elle"

Why do I get a little excited (at nearly 40 years of age) when I see the golden arches? Is it because the McDouble is the best hamburger I've ever had? Hell no! It's because there is a part of my brain that still gets excited about the toy in my happy meal! Why do I drink Budweiser or Bud Light? Well it's because frequently it's my only option. (I live in St. Louis, Missouri, which is the North American Headquarters of Anheuser-Busch InBev.) Nevertheless, the point is that if you want to appeal to all markets and everyone, or nearly everyone, then you need a massive marketing budget — which you probably don't have or you would be reading a different book. (I know you!)

Hopefully I have drilled it home to you how important it is to select a reasonably-sized niche. If you still don't agree, please re-read this section until you do. If you absolutely don't agree, you are in for a long haul.

What Size Should My Niche Be?

It should be whatever size it is. Don't worry about size — focus on how to reach your niche and how to communicate to your prospects. Are the individuals in your niche similar enough to each other that you can use common language to appeal to them?

Right Size, But Too Diverse?

If they are so diverse that you can't communicate to them in a consistent manner, then they are too diverse, maybe not too big, but too different. They need to have commonalities that you can market to and appeal to. Here are a few examples:

Example 1:

Targeted Message:
Audience: single women in their 20's who are frustrated that they don't make enough money
Message: "I can show you how to make more money, so you can buy the things you want and have leftover income to save for your wedding."

versus

Broad Message:
Audience: anyone who wants to make more money
Message: "I can help you make more money."

Example 2:

Targeted Message:

Audience: middle-aged men who work in sales and wish they had a better golf swing
Message: "I can teach you how to have a great golf swing that will help you impress clients and close more deals on the golf course."

versus

Broad Message:
Audience: anyone who wants a better golf swing
Message: "I can help you improve your golf swing."

Can you see how the tighter niche is easier to market to and how much more specific and powerful you can be in your message to them? "I can help you make more money" and "I can help you improve your golf swing" are boring, generic messages that we have heard before. Do something powerful and unique! Don't just jump into some gigantic lake that thousands of other people are competing in. It's not that it can't be done; it's that you can't AFFORD to fight and compete with the big companies and their big marketing budgets.

You might be wondering, "How the hell does he know what I can or cannot afford?" I know because I know who I wrote this book for. My reader can't afford to compete with everyone else on the planet who teaches golf. Not only do I know who is reading this book, I'm literally writing it directly to that person: YOU. Choose a niche and speak directly to them in powerful, compelling language, and you will be successful.

Common Sense Disclaimer: I know I've been saying it's not about size, but you do have to use common sense. You need to pick a niche that is large enough; in other words, there have to be an adequate number of them to actually buy enough of your product(s) to produce adequate revenue.

There is no formula to figuring this out. It does involve a little trial and error, a little common sense, and a lot of research. You just have to do the work to figure it out. Relax, think it through and you'll be fine. You will NOT get it perfect right away. You are probably going to make some changes as you go through this niche definition process. That's OK.

What Is Their View Of The World?

It's impossible to sell anything to anyone unless you have some understanding of how they view the world. How do they look at things? How do they approach problems? What do they believe as it relates to your topic?

For example, if you are teaching people about alternative medicine, you have to consider their perspective on that subject. There are people who will believe that you are a crackpot and will want nothing to do with you. Trying to market to those people would be a complete waste of your time. Thats OK; they are not your niche. When defining your niche, make sure you target people who have viewpoints that are compatible with your own, or you will have an uphill battle.

You ARE trying to change how they think, but you can't target a market that is completely closed off to your ideas. There is a little guesswork at first, but as you interact with more and more people, you will dial it in.

Where Are They?

It is important to know WHERE your niche is. Where can you find them? Are they on specific Facebook groups? This is a very different question than, "Are they on Facebook?" Everybody is on Facebook. We are asking if there are specific groups or specific places on Facebook where they hang out. Are they a member of professional or other associations? Are there certain blogs they follow or visit regularly? Do they go to clubs? This is an important part of defining your niche. You have to know WHERE they are in order to find them and market to them.

How Do I Reach Them?

It's vital that you know how to reach your niche. If you cannot reach them, you cannot connect with them, i.e. market and sell to them. How do you know how to reach them? You will have to do some research. How do you do the research? Find someone who is in your niche (perhaps an existing prospect or customer) and talk to them.

Talk to them as if they are your friends or acquaintances; talk to them online and at networking events. Getting to know your followers and prospects is the funnest part of your job!

This week alone, I'm interviewing six people in my niche. I asked if I could interview them; then offered a complimentary strategy session where I will spend one hour mapping out a customized strategy I have created just for them. Know what the best part of this is? THEY WILL ASK ME MORE QUESTIONS! I'll learn more about them. If they ask a question, that means other people in my niche probably have that same question — that becomes a point I can address in my marketing materials, products, etc. The more I know about the people in my niche, the better I can serve them, and the more they will like me.

The Business View

You need to create a view of the business aspects of your expert lifestyle. Why? Because it really IS a business. The more you treat it like one, the more successful it will be. This is really important. When you have a business plan, you have a starting point for everything you do. When you are creating something or doing some activity, be very deliberate about doing it and notice if it fits your business plan and is actually CONTRIBUTING to the goals you have laid out.

One of the best reasons for creating a business view is the "silver bullet syndrome" that is so prevalent in this industry. When you see a shiny object coming at you, you can look at it, see if it fits with your business view, and then decide if it makes sense to keep it or if you should chuck it. If you don't have a business plan, you are much more likely to become distracted by the constant barrage of shiny objects!

Two of the most important parts of your business plan are:

1. Clear goals, and
2. Clear definition of HOW you are going to make money.

Goals

I'm not trying to go into a long discussion on goal setting because there are plenty of books on the subject, but suffice it to say that setting goals is the way to get stuff done. That's a pretty universal truth, but there is another good reason why your expert lifestyle business needs to have documented goals— so you can make sure that each and every action you take is in alignment with your goals.

There are so many different things you can do, different directions you can go, etc. You have to have something to hold each of those ideas up to so you can determine if they are in alignment with your strategic plan. This will prevent you from wasting time going down a path that is cool or exciting, or worse yet, a path that some internet marketer sent you down but that doesn't align with your goals. You will STILL need a considerable amount of discipline to avoid those pitfalls, but you will never avoid them unless you have clearly-documented goals.

How You're Gonna Make Money

How are you going to make money? You'll just create some products and the cash will start flying in, right? Sorry, that's not gonna work. (I know from personal experience.) You have to have a clear strategy for how you are going to make money.

Are you going to coach one-on-one? Are you going to package and sell your knowledge in books, online training, live seminars, etc.? Are you going to use a licensing model? Are you hoping to do many different things? Most successful people do a number of different things to bring in profit, but you can't start out that way. You may have a goal to be doing eight different things in three years; that's great but you need to start with a small (more manageable) handful right now.

Two Is The Magic Number

Start with two. Two is more than one; so if one fails, you have a fallback. It's also not so many that you can't keep up with them. The important thing is that you have a clear plan for HOW to monetize your expertise and that it is focused on no more than TWO ways of making money.

I also want to be clear that this is not about creating a massive, 75-page business plan that is fit for a Harvard Business Plan contest. Your plan only needs to outline the main things that you have decided as you progress through this book.

It Must Be Written Down

Having all of this written out keeps you grounded. What would you say to an architect who said, "I don't need blueprints, it's all in my head." You'd think he's crazy! And he would be. He doesn't have time to explain all the detail of his plan to the hundreds of people who will need to see it in order to make his vision a reality. As your business grows, you will need more and more "trades" (see sidebar) to run your business. We'll talk more about that in chapter eleven.

In construction, the term "trade" is used to describe people who do specific types of activities, for example electricians, plumbers, steel workers, etc. In your expert lifestyle business, you will also need trades. These will include technologists, coaches, administrative help, accountants, etc.

It is easy to get distracted by all those great (or hair-brain) ideas that you come up with. I get lots of hair-brain ideas — I think that crazy ideas, even if they aren't practical, are an important part of the creative process. Let them flow! But, always keep looking at your Lifestyle Elevation View.

That's why I designed this step of the process — to make sure you're clear about what you are doing. I recommend reviewing your blueprints at least once a week to make sure they are always front-of-mind when working on your expert lifestyle business.

The Exception

What I just said about following your blueprints is important; however, I do need to mention that there are times when changing course is the right thing to do. I'm not saying you should never change; I am saying not to make changes "willy-nilly."

A change in course needs to be thoroughly thought-out and implemented properly, not done simply because you had a great idea, OR because you've grown tired of your current course of action. A solid blueprint takes time and patience to build and you don't want to give up on it prematurely unless you have solid, strategic reasons.

It Evolves Forever

If you are just beginning to create your expert lifestyle business, everything you have written down is just a hypothesis (and that's totally OK, you have to start with something). As you have more interaction with your followers, learn more and practice teaching more, this will get clearer and clearer. But it will ALWAYS be a work in progress. It doesn't matter how well you know your niche and your followers, you will change, they will change and the world will change. That's why NOTHING is ever permanent in your business.

Get Started! I have created worksheets you can use to write all this stuff out and they are available at:

howtoquitworkingbook.com/blueprints

Conclusion

This isn't the most exciting part of creating an expert lifestyle business, but it is DEFINITELY the most important part. Those who flounder (and I see it every day) flounder because they don't do this part. They waste time and don't get the results they want because they are not taking the creation of these blueprints seriously, or because they are skipping ahead to create some CD they are going to sell for 27 bucks. Meanwhile, they don't know who they are going to sell it to, what that person wants, or what problem they are actually solving.

Take this stuff seriously. Your business and your lifestyle depend upon it. In the next chapter, we're going to pour some concrete for your skyscraper.

Think Of It Like This:

✗ If you don't clearly define and write down what you are building and what you want it to look like, you are like an architect working without blueprints.

✗ Writing this out not only keeps you grounded, but also gives you the documents that you can then hand over to others to help you build your skyscraper.

✗ All of this information is just a hypothesis. It's always a hypothesis, and will continue to evolve and get better and better over time. Never feel like it has to be perfect.

Do It Like This:

✓ Create your blueprints, using the templates at howtoquitworkingbook.com/blueprints.

✓ Review them on a regular basis to ensure you are staying on track with your plans.

✓ Refine them as necessary when it makes good sense. They will continue to evolve as long as you have a business.

Chapter 6

Cement Your Foundation

"To put it bluntly, I seem to have a whole superstructure with no foundation. But I'm working on the foundation."
— Marilyn Monroe

I love learning about how they built something massive, like the Golden Gate Bridge, the Empire State Building or the Chunnel. I think it is amazing how such massive structures are built – even that it's possible to build them. The builders of all of these structures have one thing in common – they built a foundation first.

The Foundation Is Key

Believe it or not, the complex phase of The Lifestyle Masterplan™ is creating the foundation or base upon which the whole thing is built. It is absolutely critical to have the right foundation. You can't build the Empire State Building on mud. You can't tie the cables of the Golden Gate Bridge to a tree. You have to have a solid foundation. And that is what the first phase of The Lifestyle Masterplan™ does.

I know this from experience. I tried to build a skyscraper on mud. I tried and tried to build my following as a Do-It-Yourself home improvement expert without having an email list provider! I tried to do it without having a way to capture incoming leads, and most erroneously, without any great value piece to give away! I found out first-hand about what doesn't work. Without those basic things in place, you are just a teenager in your parent's basement. Even if you're not in your parent's basement, you might as well be.

I am intensely passionate about this. I get red-faced when working with a client and they say they want to do this and do that. I tell them, "We MUST build this foundation first, or the whole damn thing is going to come crashing down." It is a sequence. One thing comes after another. First things first. Everything in The Lifestyle Masterplan™ is designed to be done in sequence.

Don't do anything else until you build your foundation. It simply doesn't make sense to build a skyscraper on anything but solid, reinforced concrete.

In this chapter we will cover the key pieces that form the foundation of your expert lifestyle business. The Empire State Building is built on a foundation of solid concrete that's 55 feet deep. It's big and heavy and is such a solid foundation that it reaches all the way down to the granite bedrock beneath Manhattan.

Let's start pouring some concrete. Now we're going to start talking about some of the basic pieces you must put in place to have a solid foundation.

Blogging

Create a blog. On your blog you will publish great content that your followers are interested in, and MOST IMPORTANTLY, that provides VALUE! This is the first thing you should do. Create a blog and get some great content on it – start with at least six blog posts. You don't want to send people to a blog that doesn't have any content on it. That's no way to build credibility! It's a great way to get people to say, "so what?" Just bang out six blog posts. You can do that in a half day or so. In fact, you probably have already written something on your topic; so you probably have some stuff you can use with minor tweaking.

Social Media

Set up accounts on the major social media outlets. For crying out loud, don't get caught up in using every little fly-by-night social media site that comes along. As of this writing, the major social media sites that are the best use of your time are:

> Facebook
> Linkedin
> Twitter
> Pinterest
> YouTube

Forget the rest. This is where you should focus your limited time for the maximum value. You need to have some presence on all five of these, but you should focus more time/energy on only one or two of them. In the chapter seven, we will get into the specifics of what and how much you should be doing on each of these.

These accounts need to be set up first. This is an important step and is NOT HARD, if you have followed the steps so far. In chapter five, you created all the information that you will need in order to fill in the information required by these sites.

What About A Big Fancy Website?

Back in the 90's, the internet was a giant pamphlet. The great news is that it's now evolved to more than just a pamphlet. Unfortunately, there is still a misconception that spending $25K to have someone design and build a beautiful, pamphlet-style website is an effective use of your limited resources.

Save the money. Your blog is plenty for now. Most blogging platforms will allow you to create additional pages where you can display your bio, consulting rates, testimonials, product information, and all the other things you need to have publicly available. Think of your blog and website as all-in-one.

At some point on this journey, it may make sense to create a full-blown website. You may reach a point where you want to have a large, fancy, professionally-done website. That's perfectly fine and appropriate in many cases; but for the time being, it's important that you focus your limited resources where they matter most – for someone starting out and getting known, a fancy website isn't where your money is best spent.

Your Net

In order to get known for your knowledge, you have to have a net. Much of your foundation consists of the pieces designed to create and fill this net. If we were to compare it to a basketball game, the net is how you catch the "shots" you take. The shots you take are all the efforts you make to promote yourself. The shots include things like your blog posts, Facebook updates, speaking engagements, direct mail pieces, joint ventures, interviews and all the other stuff you do to get yourself known. But if you don't have a net, none of them will stick.

Let's talk about this a bit more. When you meet someone at a cocktail party and want to talk to them further (to develop a friendship, business relationship, or maybe even a romantic relationship), what do you do? You ask for their phone number, email, or maybe connect on Facebook, Linkedin, etc. You are trying to create a way or a method by which you can contact them.

If you didn't have a phone, Facebook, Linkedin, email or a fax number, you would have a really hard time remaining connected with this cool person you met. You'd have to just hope you crossed paths or you'd have to agree to meet somewhere.

Capturing a lead is just like making a basket

To continue this analogy, while you were at the party, you said some things that interested the other person. That's why they were willing to share their information with you.

That is exactly how it is when you are getting known. You need a net to capture the attention of the people you encounter AND (just as importantly) impress!

You need to have a net and some bait to attract your reader.

Let's start by talking about what you are going to use as bait to entice the reader into your net.

Your Value Piece (BAIT)

In chapter five, we talked about what you have to offer and who you offer it to. We also talked a lot about your followers and what makes them tick. Now you are going to create something that is valuable and awesome that you can give them FOR FREE.

We want this to be something that will change their lives. Something that will make them sit up and say, "Wow, if she gives this away, the stuff she charges for must be amazing!" Think about that as you go through this next step. Focus on making sure THAT is the reaction of your followers as they experience your value piece.

Based on the analysis you did in the previous section, take a look at your followers and decide what you could give them that will completely change the way they think or that will give them a whole new perspective on their situation. This is your chance to woo them big time. Develop a piece of content that will make them say WOW – that will make them go nuts for you. This is how you are going to become well-known and respected as an expert in your field.

As you think about what that value piece should be, don't overcomplicate it. A simple way to approach this is to think about what the question is that you are asked most frequently – then come up with an answer to it.

Give Away The Farm!

One of the misconceptions that causes a lot of people to create an ineffective value piece is that they are afraid to "give away the farm." I'm here to tell you to GIVE AWAY THE DAMN FARM! You might be thinking, "But if I give away this good stuff, what will I sell?" I understand your point, but let's flip it around. If you DON'T build a following, you will never SELL anything.

You could have the cure to cancer, but if you don't have a captivated list of followers, you won't sell anything. This is the time to give something really awesome that will revolutionize the topic in your prospect's mind.

People Will Still Be Hungry For More

Many of my clients fear that they will give away too much and there will be nothing left to sell. To calm your fears, remember that, as an expert, you probably don't realize how much you actually know. Even if you give away something revolutionary, there will always be a desire for more information and detail. If everyone reading this book read it 15 times and took copious notes, there would still be people calling me wanting my help. If I expanded it to double the length, people would still call me wanting help!

Even in a full-blown book, you are only going to scratch the surface of what you know. There is always more. Think of it like an apple – give away the skin; give away a few bites; there will still be a lot of the apple left to sell. And in this example, there is no limit to that apple – because once you build your following, you will have people asking you for other types of apples, oranges, bananas and so on. The possibilities are endless.

Delivering Your Value Piece

Now that we've established that the content possibilities for products are endless, let's talk about the delivery means or format. You can format your products in numerous ways – in fact you can even format the same content in different ways. Don't be afraid or worried about giving too much away. Go for broke! Give till it hurts!

Before I go into more detail on the means of delivery, I want to make a very important point: you need to choose a manner in which to deliver your content, but don't spend a crazy amount of time worrying about this. That is a trap that I see folks get caught in. They get so worried about whether it should be video or audio or e-book or whatever; they worry about what they should wear; where the video should be shot; what kind of camera is good enough. Ultimately, they waste a lot of time on this and it is less important than the content.

Focus On Your Message

Instead, focus on your message. Focus 95% of your time/attention on what you have to offer and 5% on the delivery means. Ultimately, if your message and what you are offering are solid, your means of delivery will not matter that much. In everything you do to get known for your knowledge, you want to focus more on your message and less on the means of delivering it.

Methods of Delivery for Your Value Piece

Now let's look at the 5% of your brainpower/time/attention that you are going to devote to the delivery means of your value piece. Here are the main options, along with the associated pros and cons.

E-book

This is an electronic document that is usually in a PDF format. PDF is just a standardized way of delivering documents. An e-book is a document that you write and publish; there is nothing complicated about it. Right now I'm writing this chapter in Microsoft Word. If I were to save this document as a PDF, I would have an e-book. Then I could email the PDF to you, or put it on my website, or whatever I wanted to do with it.

The key thing to understand is that it is a document that will be *read* by your followers. They will read it on their screen or they may choose to print it out.

Video

Video is becoming increasingly popular because it is effective. When I say video, I'm not talking about hiring an expensive video crew; I'm referring to a simple video that you shoot with inexpensive video equipment at your house, office or somewhere else that seems fitting.

Video can be intimidating – people are self-conscious and nervous on camera; they may worry about not getting their words right or stumbling over a word; or they may be concerned about their appearance or how their voice sounds. I want to assure you that viewers do not care how you look, how you sound or anything trivial like that. They care about the INFORMATION you are giving them; they care that you are providing VALUE. When in doubt, refer back to Rule #1 of getting known for your knowledge: "nobody cares about you." They care about the information you are providing.

Screen Capture

This is a hybrid between PDF and video – it is a PowerPoint or other type of presentation with captions, graphics and images on the screen while your voice narrates. This is very popular now. As a practical matter, consider this a video – it's a special type of video that doesn't have your face on it. Instead it has text and graphic images accompanied by your voice.

> For more information on screen flow software, go to howtoquitworkingbook.com/ screenflow

This works very well for people who are camera-shy. Because the viewer can't see you, you don't need to worry about how you look (you can do it in your underwear if you want). The really cool thing about screen capture (also called screen flows) is that you can refer to your notes as much as you want, or even read from a script.

The biggest downside is that, unlike e-books and videos, the screen capture presentation will require special software. There are a number of screen capture software programs out there; most are less than 100 bucks and are well worth the investment.

Pick One

My best advice with regard to your delivery means is to just pick one. Pick one that you are comfortable with and that makes you feel the most at ease. You could practice doing videos for days or weeks and make a really great video, but that time would probably be better spent working on creating valuable content or on promoting your brand. Take the path of least resistance; relax; do what sounds the easiest. Then focus the other 95% of your time/energy on the valuable stuff – your content.

Using Your Value Piece: Creating Your Net

To continue with the basketball analogy, what is the net? The net is your email list. Your main goal is to get email addresses onto that list. That is where your best leads will go and is the list you will use to SELL your stuff. The number of QUALITY emails you have on your list is directly proportional to the amount of product you can sell. You will sell *directly* to your email list – that's why creating your net is so important.

Everything you do should be designed to drive people to join your email list. Your promotional activities will entice readers to "get this valuable thing that will help you." In order to get it, they will have to enter their email address. Then that valuable email address will be sent to you and you've just made a 3-pointer (your mailing list).

This requires that you set up an account with a reputable email list provider. We'll discuss how to do this in a moment.

Email Address In Exchange For Value Piece

Your value piece should NOT be publicly accessible in any way. The prospect MUST enter their email address in order to get it – that's the whole point! Why? For two purposes:

1. This gets you a LEAD! You now have the email address of a person you can continue to provide value to via email, and who you will eventually sell to via that email address.
2. It also pre-qualifies them. It ensures you have only interested people on your email list. You can rest assured that no wealthy, 80-year-old, retired man signed up for your, "How to start a lawn-care business for less than 500 bucks" e-book! Only people who are interested signed up. That means you aren't wasting time on unqualified leads.

Lead Capture Page

You will need a place to send these people so they can sign up for your email list. You could send them to your website with detailed instructions on how to sign up:

"Go to www.awesomesiteaboutlovemaking.com and click on "resources," then click "free e-

*book," then enter your name and email address
for your e-book."*

OOOOOOOOOR, You could make it much easier for them to
give you their email address:

*"Go to www.awesomelovemakingsite.com/ebook
for your free e-book."*

It has to be simple. As humans, we have extremely limited
attention spans. We really do act like toddlers our entire lives!
We need to be sent to a completely distraction-free place to enter
our email address. We need to be sent to a place with no purpose
other than to enter our email address for our free e-book. We will
get distracted if there are shiny bells and whistles and other
things to click on. That's the point of a lead capture page – to
funnel prospects onto your mailing list (or into your net).

Focus On The Goal

I'm sure all of us have bought many cars in our lives, so we're all
familiar with that process. When you go to a car dealer to buy a
car, the salesman is laser-focused on getting you to buy that car.
Nothing else. That is how laser-focused your lead capture page
needs to be. Have you ever been to a dealer to buy a car, and
while he is trying to sell you the car, the salesman says, "How
would you like to flip through this gourmet cooking magazine
while we talk?" NEVER! Why? Because the car salesman wants
to keep your attention on that car (and the benefits to you)
throughout the entire conversation.

That cooking magazine is like all the other bells and whistles on
your website. It is simply another way for your visitors to get
distracted from your goal of "capturing the lead" or of getting
their email address on your mailing list.

The lead capture page is a single page on your web site that
allows your prospects to enter their email address in exchange
for their free e-book, video, or screen capture value piece. This
page will very clearly state the benefits of your value piece in

terms that resonate with your prospect. There will be a clear headline stating the benefit, along with a call to action, for example:

"Enter your email address below to learn how to get 25% better gas mileage."

Email Providers

The most important thing you can do to be successful is to begin capturing email addresses, as we discussed in the previous section. These email addresses become your prospect list. Email will be the primary way you communicate with your prospects. Most importantly, it will be the primary way you SELL to them.

You can't just go into your Hotmail or Gmail account or Microsoft Outlook and blast off an email to a huge list of people. You may be able to get away with this when you have a very small list, but this will not work as you get a bigger list. If you are reading this, you have some big goals, so position yourself NOW to meet those goals. That means get an account with a large, reputable email provider.

You Don't Want To Be Seen As Spam

This is important is because spammers have made email difficult for everyone. They have created a "guilty until proven innocent" environment. Anywhere between 70% and 90% of email sent over the internet on a daily basis is spam. So you can see why this is difficult. By sending quality information to people who have told you they want to receive it, you are in a minority, unfortunately.

When internet providers see an incoming email, they run it through a series of filters to determine if it is SPAM. They look at things like punctuation, capitalization, format of text, specific words or phrases used, etc. They know what spam usually looks like and are checking to see if your email might be spam.

The internet providers also know where spam typically comes from. Reputable email providers have policies for their users that require you to adhere to certain standards. Because the internet providers know this, they are willing to be more forgiving of emails that come from these reputable providers. In other words, they place more trust in emails coming from reputable companies like Aweber, Infusionsoft or Mailchimp. That is why you want your email coming from one of these reputable email providers.

Email Laws

There is also a considerable amount of newer legislation that you need to comply with. These reputable email providers ensure that they (and therefore you) are in compliance with the laws. I have no desire to understand or interpret those laws, which is why I leave it up to them. I'd rather focus on differentiating aspects of my business. If you use a reputable email provider and follow their terms and services, you'll be fine.

These providers are not expensive. They start around 20 bucks a month. Generally the price goes up as you build a larger list. In other words, the more email addresses you have on your list, the more they charge you. The

For more information on email providers, please visit:

howtoquitworkingbook.com/email

great thing about this pricing model is that your price increases as your list grows, and as your list grows, so does your income, which makes the additional expense totally worth it!

Conclusion

That's it for the first phase of The Lifestyle Masterplan™. But we're just getting started. Now that we've poured this 55 foot deep concrete foundation, we can start building that massive following that will be the key to your success. Don't start trying to engage people until you have done this foundational piece. I cannot emphasize how incredibly important it is.

Now let's start building your skyscraper.

Think Of It Like This:

- ✗ If you don't have a solid foundation, you won't have a business, and you won't create the lifestyle you want.
- ✗ Put these foundational pieces in place first. Take time to get them right, but not perfect. You will refine as you learn more.
- ✗ Giving away great, quality information is how you gain credibility and build your following, so do it with pleasure and enthusiasm!

Do It Like This:

- ✓ Create a value piece that is AWESOME and transforms the way your prospects think about your topic.
- ✓ Sign up with an email provider.
- ✓ Set up your blog and social media profiles.

Chapter 7

Erect Your Structure

"I like thinking big. If you're going to be thinking anything, you might as well think big."
— Donald Trump

I originally called this step of The Lifestyle Masterplan™ "Promote" because that's exactly what it it. "Promote" is the marketing word, but in this industry it's less about promotion and more about actually creating a connection with your followers by providing them with valuable information. In turn, they will come to know you, trust you, and be ready to BUY from you.

This step of the process is by far the most labor-intensive. It's probably not the hardest, but it definitely requires the most work. It is also the most fun! You are building a business around something you LOVE, so you're definitely going to have fun talking about it and creating that deep connection with people who also care about what you are doing. That's your marketing! Creating a connection with people while you are helping them with something you really care about. Didn't I tell you this is the best industry ever?

Now we are actually BUILDING the passionate, engaged group of followers who will buy your products/services. This group of people, that I call your followers (also commonly called your list, tribe, crew, herd, etc. depending on the guru), is exactly what will set you apart from everyone else who has a "great idea."

Think of this passionate, engaged group of followers like the catalyst that will push your business to the highest levels possible. More, deeper connections push your skyscraper higher and higher into the air. In the next chapter, we'll raise the spire to the top of that skyscraper.

Empire State Building, rising to the 102nd Floor.

The most important thing I have learned about business in general is that great ideas are a dime a dozen. Everybody has a genius inspiration. Some of them are great ideas, while some are dumb ideas that seemed good after a few cocktails. Most are somewhere in between. The point is that the human brain has no trouble coming up with lots of amazing ideas when we get in the right, creative headspace. What sets successful people apart from everyone else is their ability to EXECUTE those ideas. And when I say execute, I really mean market.

Here is the worst thing anyone can say to you in this business: "You are the best-kept secret in your field." Translation: "You suck at marketing."

That's harsh; but it's true. Forget the ideas, forget the products; create the connection. Those connections are the force that pushes you upward. And since your reading this book, you're gonna be just fine, because I'm showing you exactly how to do it.

Case in point -- how many conversations have you had that went something like this:

> *Friend: I have the most amazing idea. I have an idea for a <<gadget, product, service>> that I think is just incredible, and it's going to change the world.*

> *You know how everyone struggles with <<some thing that may or may not be a struggle>> all the time? Well, I thought of this <<gadget, product, service>> that will totally eliminate that struggle. Isn't that fantastic?*

> *You: Wow! That IS a great idea. I struggle with that every day. Just the other day, I <<fill in example>>.*

> *Friend: My mom, husband, and sister-in law all think it's a genius idea. I just don't know how to get started.*

> *You: That's frustrating. It's such a great idea!*

If I had a nickel for each time I've had that conversation, I'd be writing this from my villa in St. Bart's. I don't participate in those conversations. Instead I refer them to this book and show them a better way!

The problem here is that this great idea is ahead of the buyer's need or want (or their understanding of their need or want). Too many people believe that if you have a great idea, people will beat down your door to buy it. They won't – great idea or not. The truth is they will not beat down your door at all.

Is your idea a great one? Who knows? There are too many factors that go into a buying decision to know that. Getting a great idea in the shower or while you drive to work is fine, but it's not taking into consideration the infinite number of thoughts and factors that go through a person's head when deciding to buy or not.

The effective way is to:

1. Build a following first by providing great free information
2. Ask them what they want
3. Sell them what they just told you they want

So, you create a relationship with them, ask what they want, they tell you, and you create it. NOW, they will beat down your door! Why? Because you have EXACTLY WHAT THEY JUST TOLD YOU THEY WANT! Wouldn't you buy – wouldn't you buy a product that was custom-designed to be exactly what you told someone you wanted? Of course you would. This is so awesome.

To be clear, I'm not suggesting you should create a separate product for each person – that would be insane. You will create products and services based on the aggregate information you receive from your followers. Then you will continue to refine that based on the feedback you receive. We'll talk in chapter eight about how to create products that keep giving you feedback so you can keep moving closer and closer to and addressing more and more of your followers' needs.

The Housekeeping Of Your Expert Lifestyle Business

There are certain things you will need to do in your business on a regular basis, just like in your personal life. In your life there are daily or weekly or monthly activities that just have to be done, such as:

- pay your bills
- clean the bathroom
- buy groceries
- brush your teeth
- wash your car
- cook dinner

These things don't excite you, entertain you, or take you to the next level in life, but they do need to be done. Sometimes we pay other people to do these things or we share the responsibility with a spouse or significant other – both are also options for how you might handle these housekeeping activities in your expert lifestyle business.

Just like paying bills and cleaning the bathroom, there are certain things that are baseline housekeeping activities; in other words, things that everyone building an expert lifestyle business must do in order to succeed. These things will get your name out and build up your following.

Here are some of the main housekeeping activities:

1. Stay in tune with the news in your topic area
2. Build relationships with other experts in your industry
3. Provide valuable free content via your blog, social media and email

Let's delve into each of these in a little more detail.

Stay In Tune With The News In Your Topic Area

Being recognized as an expert requires, first and foremost, actually BEING an expert! That means staying on top of what is going on in your subject area.

- What research is being done?
- What are people talking about?
- What events are going on?
- What new information has been published in books, websites and journals?

Not only is staying current a part of having your thumb on your industry, but it also gives you great content to publish for your followers, which in turn further builds your credibility as a source of industry expertise and knowledge.

It's imperative that you know all the major media outlets for your industry and keep up-to-date with them. Get connected to them electronically and check them regularly. Subscribe to the journals, magazines, blogs, etc.

To automate this process, set up an RSS reader with all the news sources from your topic area. It will tell you what is new and give you links to articles. This will become part of your process as you'll be checking in and reading the latest industry information a few times a week.

> RSS Reader: An RSS reader isn't some super-fancy techie thing for geeks; it's just a tool that consolidates all of your news sources into a single summarized page. I use Google's RSS reader at reader.google.com.

This part is no joke. People will come to rely on you for your perspective and opinions on your topic area and you owe it to them to be on top of it. Stay current. If you don't, you won't last.

Build Relationships In Your Industry

Relationships are how this whole thing works. The relationships I have worked very hard to build are responsible for most of my business. You must set aside a specific time for relationship-building each and every day. Set a goal, such as each day contact three new people; then reach out and offer them something of value to start building the relationship.

Now I want to be really clear about your objective. By doing this relationship-building work, you will probably get clients, either directly or through referrals, and that is awesome. You just can't talk to that many people without converting a few, but the true goal of building these relationships is not to get clients for your business. The ultimate goal is to build relationships with influential people in your field. These relationships will be a key avenue for you to get your message out.

Make sure you subscribe to these folks' email lists, read their blogs, follow them on social media, etc. to learn what they are about. Follow them and connect on social media. This helps to build the relationship and teaches you more about them.

Why is this important?
The blunt truth here is that you are trying to get access to their audiences. For example, if you are a golf swing expert, you would reach out to other golf experts, people who own golf stores, people who publish golf newsletters, people who write or blog about golf, etc. The way you do this is to build rapport with them slowly. Start with an email, phone call or social media message that offers them something of value, such as help or advice, a guest blog post, etc. You might offer to be interviewed, interview them, or just exchange ideas about your topic area. Another great way to get their attention is to buy their products. That definitely gets their attention!

Now that we've established the goal of these contacts, it is very important to reach out to the right people. When allocating your precious time, you'll want to spend more of it on those people who can help you. The bottom line is that you want to connect with people who *actually have an audience* that you can eventually get access to and sell to.

The best way to determine if they have an audience is to go to the person's website and see if they are collecting emails. In other words, check to see if their website asks for visitors' emails for a newsletter subscription or other freebie. If it does, then they will likely have an audience that they are able to reach. It's also very easy to look at their social media channels and see how many people are following them.

Provide Valuable Free Content

At the core of positioning yourself as an expert is one very simple thing: providing awesome FREE content. Your content is what will set you apart from others in your field, and MOST IMPORTANTLY, will get you the CREDIBILITY that you want and deserve. You must provide free content with value on a regular and consistent basis. When you are not marketing and selling products, you will probably be creating content for your followers. Did I mention it needs to be awesome, valuable content? OK, good.

Now let's talk about HOW you are going to actually deliver this regular content to your followers. But first, I want to be really clear that there is generally ONLY ONE reason you should engage in any type of correspondence with your followers – and that is to provide value to them.

It is okay to occasionally share something personal, wish your followers a happy holiday, or send other communications that build rapport, but they should be the exceptions. Those types of messages are best delivered in conjunction with value of some kind.

Blog

The best way to start creating regular content is to write blog posts. Write one per week. You can get administrative help for this or you can write several posts in one day and schedule them to go out automatically. None of the logistics of HOW you get it done are important. The important thing is that once a week your followers see valuable new blog content.

That NEW blog content will teach your followers something. You want readers to look at it and have a good reason to read it. Never forget how busy people are – make it worth their while to stay current on your blog posts.

Blogging is an easy and effective way of getting known to a large audience. Blogs do well in search engines; they offer a quick, easy, cheap way to get information out to a large number of people on a frequent basis. They are also a great way to showcase your knowledge and provide value to your growing audience. In addition, every time someone lands on your blog they will be asked to join your list and receive your value piece. Plus, a blog provides you with content to publish to social media – and it's not only valuable content, it's also self-promoting. It's a great one-two punch – you are providing value to your audience and promoting yourself at the same time!

Social Media

Provide content on your topic regularly. You will offer both content created by you and content created by other people. This is easy to do when you are staying in touch with what is going on in your industry (as we discussed above). Remember all those articles you are reading? They are instant social media posts! When you write a blog post, be sure to put a link to that post on social media. This doesn't take long, but gets you name recognition and develops your status as an authority in your field.

I am not talking about posting about your kids, grandkids or dog – unless those are your area of expertise. Post quality content about your area of expertise. Post a small amount of your own stuff that you have created, and a larger amount (majority) of good solid stuff that other people have created, accompanied by your unique perspective on what they wrote. For example, a good social media post might look like this:

> *The latest research on the psychology of entrepreneurship is on target. I've seen these*

principles   consistently   with   my   clients.
http://linktoreallycoolarticle.com

A post like this provides content, builds credibility, and brands you in the process. Now do that 14 times a week. Create 14 social media updates per week and schedule them to go out with an automatic scheduler, two a day for a week. Then you are finished creating content for the week! There is no better feeling than being done with social media for another week.

> To learn how to get your social media efforts completed in less than one hour a week, visit: howtoquitworkingbook.com/socialmedia

Email

As you begin collecting email addresses, you will also start to communicate with these people via email. A good way to start is with a weekly email announcing that your newest blog post is available. If you are on my list, you will notice that every Monday you receive an email with my latest blog post and video. If you are not on my list, you can join at howtoquitworkingbook.com and you will see how I deliver content via email.

The most important thing to remember is the subject line. Everyone gets a LOT of email these days and we're all busy, so many emails get deleted or skipped over. Your subject line is the "headline" of your email, and it is generally the only thing people will read before determining if they are going to open it. Therefore you must write a compelling headline. Make it something that will engage and intrigue your reader, so they WANT to open your email and get the information.

There is a lot of information out there on how to write subject lines that get opened. There is a lot that can be said about this, but I do know that just being very open and honest about what value you are providing in the email is best. Many email marketers will try to shock their readers with headlines like, "My plane went down" or "Your business is going to fail in the next

12 months." This is just crying wolf and probably *will* be very effective a few times, but then nobody will believe a thing you say in your email subjects. And it won't take long. They'll figure you out and quit opening your emails. Just be open and candid about what's in the email and be really proud of it.

Don't Screw It Up

If you do these steps correctly, you will have a group of people who genuinely like you, want to read what you send them, and most importantly, will buy from you. But don't let that go to your head. You don't EVER want to let it go to your head, but most importantly, not at first. Keeping your ego in check is critical.

You must tell yourself that no matter how much these people LOOOOOOVE you, you are a small part of their lives. They like the content you provide, they may like you as a person, some may want to meet you if given the opportunity, soon some will be eager to buy from you. They will likely forgive you for mistakes and shortcomings, but they WILL go away if you stop providing them with what they want. Always remember, it is about what THEY want, not what you want nor what you want them to want.

This is why your content needs to be razor-sharp, highly-valuable, entertaining, and written specifically for your followers' interests and needs. The best way to accomplish this is to be yourself. More specifically "be yourself on topic." Don't be yourself off-topic; that doesn't work. Again, your audience is following you for one reason – because of the quality content you provide.

Why The Lifestyle Masterplan™ Is Different (and Works)

I tell clients to be open and candid about their mistakes and shortcomings. So I will do the same. Being open and honest about your mistakes and shortcomings is how you build rapport, so I'm going to build some rapport now!

When I discovered the concept of information marketing and decided that it was a great fit (actually the only fit) for me, I started off by trying to get known as a DIY (Do-It-Yourself) home improvement expert. But I had no earthly idea what I was doing! I began by limiting my efforts to just a few things:

- Blogging
- Facebook
- Twitter
- Article Marketing
- Video Marketing
- Writing a Book
- Selling T-shirts (I have no idea why I thought this was going to work, but I think it had something to do with a conversation I had at a bar)
- Having a massive, awesome website with lots of bells and whistles
- I'm probably forgetting about 15 other things

Bear in mind, at the same time I was working a full-time, high-stress corporate job AND starting my other business in real-estate. It's probably no surprise that I hardly EVER did my housekeeping activities consistently!

How many of the things on my list do you think I actually got done? And more importantly, how many of those things do you think I did WELL and CONSISTENTLY? If you guessed NONE, you are absolutely right. A normal, reasonable person can only do so many things. I'm not normal or reasonable, but I still couldn't get it done!

It's true that in life that when we focus on too many things, we end up doing none of them well and getting poor (or no) results across the board. It's only when we limit our focus to a reasonable number of activities that we are able to accomplish something meaningful.

Why did I do all those things? (or "try to do them")?

I thought I had to.

We are constantly bombarded with marketing messages about the "next big thing." We are repeatedly told:

- You NEED TO be on Twitter
- You NEED TO have products
- You NEED TO be speaking
- You NEED TO blog
- You NEED TO be on Linkedin

So of course you think you need to do all those things. You are continually barraged with marketing messages that say,

"How I made a gazillion dollars on Twitter"
or
"How I blogged my way to a Lamborghini"
or
"How to speak for the big bucks."

Again, these can all be effective strategies, it's just that you can't (and probably don't want to) attempt them ALL.

That is where The Lifestyle Masterplan™ is different. In The Lifestyle Masterplan™, you will focus on creating the support structure that will ensure your success. First you lay a foundation, and then you build a framework. Then you will choose one or two main promotional strategies to focus on. And you'll implement those consistently and with high quality.

In the last few chapters, you got clear on the "what" or the foundation.

- Who are you?
- What do you offer?
- Who do you offer it to?

You also built your social media profiles, set up your online stuff, and created a value piece to give away. Congrats – you have poured a solid foundation on which to build this skyscraper!

The 55-foot-deep foundation you created in the previous chapters is absolutely essential, but won't do anything for you in and of itself. Next it is time to start erecting the framework for this skyscraper.

The Final Step: Connectors

In order to build a large following, the type of following that will take your expert lifestyle business to the 102nd floor, you need to put the rest of this skyscraper in place. As you know, this book isn't about hype, fluff, or any of that. It's about putting a solid foundation in place, building a strong structure and then going as high as you want. We can't do that unless we get serious and real.

If done correctly and efficiently, the housekeeping activities described previously can be done in about one hour a day, five days a week. If you've done everything up to this point, you are in an absolutely amazing place. You have great content going out to an engaged audience on a regular basis. You have a place to send people to get more (free) information about you and your area of expertise. It's seriously a great position to be in, and one that very few people are in, even after being at it for several years.

BUT, to take your expert lifestyle business to new heights, you need something more. And this is where I see so many folks get tripped up. Most people who are serious about growing their expert lifestyle business will actively seek out ways to do so. As you know, there are plenty of ways and plenty of people who will teach you. However, this is the trap that many people unwittingly fall into – thinking they have to do EVERYTHING. You don't. And if you try to, you will fail.

The Steel Connectors

When steelworkers put a piece of steel in place on a skyscraper, they put a particular piece of steel exactly where they do because the architect did all the structural calculations and made the determination that that specific piece of steel needed to be a certain size and needed to go exactly where it goes. The steelworker did not just see a cool piece of steel and thought it might be fun or look cool on the building somewhere. Experience, mandated building standards, and math all told the architect (who told the steelworker through the blueprints) where it needed to go.

The methods you use to build your following also need to be carefully calculated to ensure that they provide the support that is needed. I've done all the calculations for you. I've seen it done many different ways. I've seen it succeed and I've seen it fail. And what I know from all of my experience is that you need exactly two steel connectors to build your following.

What I mean by that is that you need two major promotional methods or strategies, which I'll call your *connectors*. These are things that you can put in place in addition to (on top of) your housekeeping activities, and these two things will seriously kick your expert lifestyle business into high gear.

I'm talking about the major things you will do (in addition to the housekeeping items) to build that connection with your followers and build your list. Let's talk about some examples.

Your Options
OK, now let's talk about some of the options for your connectors. There are a lot to choose from, but I'll hit the main ones here. By the time I finish typing the draft of this chapter, there will be ten new ones invented and 25 products offering to teach you each one. Good luck keeping up with all that. Don't try, there's not enough liquor. Here are some of the main connectors:

- Write a Book
- Create a Podcast or Web TV Show
- Blog
- Speak in Public
- Video Marketing
- Social Media

• Webinars

By no means is this an exhaustive list; there are an unlimited number of ways to promote yourself. You won't have any trouble finding other techniques or people to teach you how to implement promotional strategies.

We're going to take a look at some of the most popular strategies.

Write a Book

Writing a book is an awesome way to become known for your expertise. Spoiler alert: that's why I wrote this book! Having a book can give you instant credibility. Books live forever. Your book will probably be passed on to others many times, each time garnering more credibility for you. If nothing else, having a book shows that you actually took the time to write down some of what you know – that alone is a huge demonstration of your commitment to your field. (I know first hand, it's a lot of work!)

> I don't want to get into all the ins and outs of self-publishing vs. traditional publishing, but I will point you to this resource: howtoquitworkingbook.com/writeabook

There are a few downsides. One is the lead time. Your book offers virtually no promotional benefit while you are writing it. You don't get an ounce of recognition until it's finished and published. As of the time I'm writing this initial draft, I am about three months into writing this book and have at least another three to go before I have a full-length draft. Then there is editing, publishing, cover creation, etc. From concept to the shelf, you're looking at at least eight months, and that's if you self-publish and move really fast.

Create a Podcast or Web TV Show

It's so cool that you can literally have your own web TV or radio show up and running in minutes! This can be a great way to build credibility, relationships, and a following in your niche. And it's fun!

You can interview people in your field, interview clients, or create a show about anything that would be of interest to your niche. It's very important that whatever type of show you do is congruent with your audience's interests and needs. They have to see the benefit in it, want to watch it or listen, and receive real value from it. When these criteria are met, your podcast or web TV show will be a powerful lead-building source.

Blog

Everyone should blog (as I described in the Housekeeping Activities section). What I'm talking about now is "uber-blogging" – this is more than the one blog a week that I recommend as a baseline housekeeping activity. This is making blogging an integral part of your strategy. That means blogging more frequently, as well as working much harder to build an audience. This is a connector strategy where you are becoming a very serious blogger and are using it as one of your core strategies to build your following.

Speak in Public

Sort of like blogging, everyone in this business needs speaking skills because you will find yourself speaking at some point or another. But you can also choose speaking as one of your two major promotional strategies (connectors). You promote yourself as a speaker and spend lots of time speaking. You get to interact with large groups of your followers in "real time," gauge their reactions, and get to know them. This is time-consuming, requires travel (usually) and getting booked on the schedule for other people's events. But it is an incredibly powerful way to build your following because every single person who hears you becomes an instant lead. I don't know of any other way to get an instant captive audience.

Video Marketing

Again, everyone should be doing video to some degree. But you can also take video to the next level by creating LOTS of video and promoting it heavily. Many people say "video is hot now," and although I can't stand hype, they are right. Online video is not a fad; it's here to stay. It's not new either. We've embraced video as a communication medium since the 1950's. It's just more accessible now and is delivered online instead of over the airwaves.

Video is an important and powerful medium. Everyone should use it to some degree, but you can use it to a huge degree if you choose it as one of your two key strategies (connectors). If you're considering video, remember that while it's fun, it's also time-consuming to create, edit and publish. And video editing is one of the most expensive things you can outsource.

Social Media

I advise clients to get their social media done in one hour a week (that is, the social media efforts that are part of your housekeeping activities). And interestingly enough, from the social media efforts you implement as part of your housekeeping activities, you'll get 80% of your social media results! This is why I don't encourage people to use social media as one of their two promotional strategies (connectors) – why put in any more effort or focus when you're already getting 80% of the results from your housekeeping activities!?

Having said that, social media is a viable option for one of your two promotional strategies (connectors) if you are drawn to it and feel that you are skilled at it. If you do choose social media

> "If social media is changing your life, you're on it too much." – Jeff Steinmann, August 2011

as a connector, you will spend considerably more time on it in order to build a following. Many people have done this successfully; however, most folks simply don't want to spend that much time on social media. They want to get it done and move on. There are a lot of people out there who will tell you that social media is going to change your life. It can. But it takes a lot of time.

Webinars

Webinars are live presentations over the web. You will also hear people say that webinars are "hot" right now, and while that's true, let's put it into perspective. Webinars are one more way for you to demonstrate your knowledge in a live, interactive format. Demonstrating something live is not a new strategy. Webinars are just a modern way of delivering a live demonstration via the web.

You can do a live webinar a few times a week, or on some regular basis, on your topic area. This will be fun; you'll become polished as you do more events; and it will do great things to build your following. Just remember, it's a live demonstration or presentation delivered over the web, not a new strategy.

Which Two Should I Pick?

All these things sound great, so how do you go about picking your two connectors?

I love the answer to this question. The answer is: pick ones that you like.

If you hate writing, for goodness sake, don't make writing a book a core part of your strategy! If you love talking to people, a podcast where you interview people in your field sounds like a great way to go. This is one of the greatest things about making a living with what you know – you not only do what you want, but you also get to do it how you want. You get to pick TWO connectors for building your business, things that you like and enjoy doing. Pretty cool, huh?

You have a ton of options to choose from. The ones I listed previously are only a few of the more common ones. You can and will find plenty more options, but the important thing is to only choose two, and really focus on them. Really, really pour yourself into those two strategies (connectors) and don't be distracted by "new ideas" or the latest hype.

The Biggest Mistake

The most challenging part of this is that once you have your two connectors, you need to confidently ignore the newest, latest gimmicks and hype that come at you. Keep your head down and focus on your strategies.

Imagine how silly (not to mention expensive and dangerous) it would be if an architect changed the structural support system of a skyscraper in the middle of construction? Wow, that would be nuts! So, don't do it in your expert lifestyle business.

The most important thing to remember is that you have to stick with a strategy in order for it to work. Too many times, I see clients expect fast results from an approach, they don't see results as fast as they had hoped, and then move on to the next "big thing." They are then left with an abandoned, partially-executed strategy that simply needed more time to work and they are usually 2000 bucks poorer. Wait, I mean 1997 bucks poorer.

Patience is very important in this industry! Nothing happens overnight, despite the stories so many gurus tell. Abandoning your solid, well-thought-out strategy for something that is NEW and flashy will cause you to remain in the same rut forever.

Focusing on Two Connectors Works

Many people have done this with great success. In fact, many of the people who have successfully used these techniques to build their expert lifestyle business now have another expert business: teaching you how to do the thing that made them successful! This focused approach worked for them, not because it is a silver bullet, but because they put a lot of FOCUS on it. They poured a ton of time and energy into just (one or) TWO strategies (connectors). For example:

- Gary Vaynerchuck used video and Twitter (garyvaynerchuk.com)
- David Siteman Garland created his own online interview show (therisetothetop.com)
- Lisa Sasevich focused on speaking (lisasasevich.com)

And while each of these people did other things too, what made them successful and catapulted them to success was their FOCUS on one or two key strategies.

As I mentioned, successful people frequently start a second business that teaches you how they succeeded with their chosen technique. And in most cases, they do a great job of teaching the technique that worked for them and they offer valuable products. When you choose the promotional methods that work for you, I highly encourage you to buy products, training or coaching on those techniques. What I don't encourage is the idea that these things will change your life or change your business by themselves. They will only do that if you implement them as part of a carefully-thought-out plan.

There Is No Silver Bullet!

The pattern that I fell into, as others so often do, is believing that one technique is a silver bullet that is going to change your business. Too many times, people buy the "blog your way to riches" product, try the techniques, and get lackluster (or no) results. Then they are left broken, disappointed, and 1997 bucks poorer. So they move on to try the next technique. Next they buy the "how I retired with Facebook ads" product, but get the same result.

This approach doesn't work for two reasons:

1. They didn't pour their foundation first.
2. They didn't stick with it long enough.

We've already covered how to lay your foundation as an expert (see chapter six for more on building your foundation), so let's look at the second reason. This is called good old-fashioned "sticking with it." The big promises of fast riches and fame don't help, because it comes down to the simple fact that so much of getting known for your knowledge is a direct result of your consistency and persistency. You have to keep at it.

When we don't see results instantly, sometimes we lose patience. I'm definitely guilty of that. The fact is that the daily and weekly housekeeping activities can get boring no matter how much you enjoy your area of expertise. The best way to fix that is by building systems that automate and outsource the most repetitive tasks – we'll talk more about that in chapter eleven.

Face it – there will always be some annoying, boring stuff that has to get done. It's a matter of having the self-discipline to push through what we don't want to or feel like doing. In my *heavily-biased* opinion, THIS is the best business to be in; but like everything, there are downsides. Successful people push through the less exciting aspects in order to make their way to bigger and better things. But the best answer is to get other people to do that boring, annoying junk.

Stay Focused

I'm not saying to keep your head in the sand, but 95% of your focus needs to be on YOUR area of expertise, not on the latest online marketing, promotional or sales technique. Over time, the methods you use may change. You will review your approach (at least) every three months to ensure that it is still working for you and that you are focusing on the most appropriate strategies for you and your business.

For example, conducting complimentary strategy sessions for potential prospects is a valuable thing to do during your start-up phase; but as your business progresses, this can become overly time-consuming. As you gain credibility and awareness, you will need to put your focus in other places, and won't have the extra time to spend on less-effective techniques like complimentary sessions. That's okay. It's fine to make a change as you identify strategies (connectors) that are no longer working or that need to be adapted to accommodate your business' growth. It is NOT okay to make a change when you haven't fully executed your existing strategy and are looking for a silver bullet that will work faster.

Build Deeper Connections With Coaching Or Consulting

No matter which two heavy-hitter strategies (connectors) you choose, now you're going to get your hands really dirty as you get "up close and personal" with your followers. The purpose of this is to get to know them REALLY well, to understand on a deep level what they worry about, what their goals and aspirations are, and what makes them tick. This understanding is pivotal to successfully implementing your strategies and building your skyscraper higher.

The best way to do this is by offering coaching or consulting, either one-on-one or in a group. You have expert knowledge and people obviously need it. They would love to have time with you to learn more about what you know, and to get specific, individualized advice on how your knowledge applies to their personal situation.

Complimentary Strategy Sessions

You can get this off the ground by offering complimentary strategy sessions. I highly recommend getting some training or coaching on selling if you've never done it before. It is not hard, but does require some skills and practice to use it effectively. It will probably be the most valuable skill you ever obtain.

Consider offering brief (15 minutes or less) consultation or session on Fivver (fiverr.com). Fiverr is a site that allows you to sell products and services for five dollars. I'm not suggesting this as a revenue generating strategy, just as a way to get some personal interaction with your niche. If you do what you do well, you'll get good testimonials through Fiverr's built in rating system.

Note: If you already have a coaching or consulting practice, great! You can skip this step (or keep doing it), but read the rest of this section to make sure you are gathering the right information from your clients.

Generally it's not a good idea to offer your services for free, because you typically get little to no commitment from the "potential customer" who sought out free help. But, if you absolutely must, go ahead and offer free coaching or consulting or services to your followers in order to gather in-depth information about their preferences, needs and desires. After all, doing a few free sessions is better than not obtaining the information you need.

Why this Approach is Important…

I can't emphasize enough how important it is to gather good information! You cannot effectively market or sell to your followers if you don't have a deep understanding of them and what is important to them. Take this step very seriously. Take good notes when you talk to your followers, consolidate your notes, extract the themes, and refer to your notes often.

Hustle

It takes "hustle" to build these relationships. This step isn't only about building an email list to sell to (although it does do that), it's also about putting in place an appropriate avenue for selling your higher-priced products and services. A complimentary call is the perfect opportunity to sell a follower your individual coaching or consulting, high-priced seminars, or other products that offer a lot of personal interaction. You MUST have these kinds of relationships FIRST, in order to understand how to position and market your expertise. And you build these relationships with HUSTLE. Work your butt off for these people and give them huge value, so later you can sell them crazy, incredibly awesome value.

This approach gives you the opportunity to practice talking to your niche about your area of expertise, and provides you with opportunities to practice teaching as well.

Listen

Most importantly, you will listen to your followers. Listen to their questions and concerns. What are you saying that really resonates with them? What are you saying that makes them say, "huh?" I've gotten plenty of those huh's. It's these conversations that have led to the creation of The Lifestyle Masterplan™. You are learning how to talk to your followers. One of the things I learned early on in the complimentary sessions I gave was that the people I talked to wanted a "strategy." They didn't call it a framework, they didn't call it a plan – they called it a strategy. So I've been using that word in my marketing ever since.

Refine Your Niche

This is also going to help you refine the niche that you hypothesized when you created your initial set of blueprints. You will learn a great deal about the people you are serving. There will be trends and themes that you'll notice. You might find that a lot of unemployed lawyers are approaching you, or maybe you are really connecting well with women in their late 20's, or maybe divorced fathers are getting a lot from your teachings. Whatever the themes and trends are, you will find out while you are talking and listening (and listening and listening) to your followers.

> Did I say listen? Listen to everything your followers say. They are giving you gold. Write it down, reread it when you are writing marketing materials, and use their words to talk to them.

Get Testimonials

Whether you sell them something or not, you've provided value. Great value. Now you can ask for a testimonial. Testimonials are VERY important and are valuable assets that you need to build your business. They are one of the key foundational pieces for being successful. Obviously if you are already coaching or consulting, you will have at least a few of these on-hand.

The Desired Outcome

The amount of time you'll spend and how much interviewing and gathering of information that you'll need to do will vary. If you are someone who has been offering your services for a few years, you may have already gotten the testimonials, knowledge and experience that you need. If you are just starting out in your field (that you are already knowledgable in), then you will need to spend more time on this step.

Jeff Engaging Directly and Personally

I can't tell you exactly how much to do. But I can tell you what you want the outcome to be. You are hoping to achieve the following:

1. *An understanding of who your target is* and what makes them tick. (Can you think of a better way to do this than by *talking* to them?)
2. *Build your credibility.* Not only are we talking about obtaining testimonials, but we're also talking about gathering success stories. You want to be able to say, "I helped so-and-so achieve xxx result."
3. *Practice teaching your followers.* Learn how to teach them by actually teaching them. There is no better way to do this than by talking one-on-one with them – actually ASKING questions and LISTENING to what they say.

But I Don't Want To Do Consulting Or Coaching…

Too bad! This is not the silver bullet, "it's easy, just go do it" book; there are plenty of those. I'm telling you the truth. And the fact is you have to engage with people to learn about them. If you can come up with another way to meet the same objectives, go for it. The important thing is that you get the outcomes I listed above.

One-on-one coaching or consulting is not part of my long-term strategy, so I only do a small amount of it and it's very expensive; but I will always do some because it's that important to stay engaged with your followers if you want to continue to serve them in a valuable way. This means you have to stay engaged on a deeper level than Facebook, Twitter or blog comments allow.

Integrating This Practice Into Your Marketing

Coaching or consulting will not be your primary lead generation method for building your email list, but it does serve that purpose too. Every person who enters this process won't end up receiving a complimentary session or becoming your client, but you will build in invitations for people to join your mailing list into every step of this process.

The phrase "Go sign up for my email list" is absolute profanity in my book!

Here's a much more compelling way to word your invitation:

"If you liked <whatever you just provided>, go to www.myawesomething.com to get an awesome free resource."

Connecting Works

When you follow The Lifestyle Masterplan™ and do these steps thoughtfully, you will have a leg up on most people in this industry. While this step of connecting with your followers is not hard, it is the most critical part of building your business. The way this ACTUALLY works is that you FIRST build a group of passionate, engaged followers and THEN you find out what they want, and THEN you sell it to them. The Lifestyle Masterplan™ is really pretty simple – if you don't have the connections, then you won't make the sales.

Now let's talk about the next phase, raising the spire on your building to awesome heights (and making money)!

Think of It Like This:

- ✗ Creating a connection with your niche *is* your marketing. It's absolutely the most important thing you do.
- ✗ Every touchpoint you have with your niche is an opportunity to learn more about them and build relationships.
- ✗ Engaging directly and personally with your niche is the best way to get to know them, so you can market to them.

Do It Like This:

- ✓ Provide free content via blog, social media and email.
- ✓ Build relationships with others in your industry.
- ✓ Pick and implement two heavy-hitter strategies (connectors).
- ✓ Build a deep understanding of your audience with coaching or consulting.

Chapter 8

Raise Your Spire

"I wish developing great products was as easy as writing a check. If that was the case, Microsoft would have great products."
— Steve Jobs

The number and types of information products that you can create for relatively little cost are absolutely limitless. There are e-books, print-on-demand books, CD training, DVD training, seminars, teleseminars, etc. Unfortunately, there are a lot of people out there teaching about product creation, when what you really need as you are building an expert lifestyle business is a following to tell you *what* to create. Then the actual product creation part is as EASY as falling off a log.

That is why this section is fairly short, as compared to the others. When you get to this point, you have done most of the hard work already!

My clients are always full of ideas.

> "I want to create a six-part daily meditation CD!"
> "I should write a book and sell it for Kindle!"
> "I want to do a weekend retreat and sell it for 2500 dollars!"

My answer is always the same.

1. Build a following first.
2. Create a connection with them and find out what they want.
3. Then you create exactly what they just told you they want and sell it to them.

They see products, and then dollar signs. Don't get me wrong, I'm in this industry for several reasons, and money is certainly not the least of them! There is nothing wrong with dollar signs, but this approach is simply backwards. You have a ton of awesome tools at your disposal to use to build a following. They will tell you what they want and need and then you simply create it. The creation of those products is absolutely the easiest part. Everything we've done up to this point is to build that following.

You Can't Sell A Hypothesis

When you have a great product idea BEFORE you have developed a following that might be good content for a value piece or other free content giveaway, because all it really is is a HYPOTHESIS until you have found out if it's a good fit for your future followers.

It is easy to get into the old chicken-and-egg situation. I can hear you now, "But Jeff, didn't you tell me a few chapters ago, that I needed to create something to give away for free in order to build my list?" YES, I did! And if you have a great idea for something to create before having a following, that's great; but make that your FREE value piece that you give away. Don't start thinking about products (to sell) just yet. Investing a lot of time and money into something people MAY OR MAY NOT buy is simply a recipe for wasted time. Identify a need first, then fill the need; rather than getting a brilliant idea and then trying to force it into a market that may or may not want it.

You may have already created something and can't get it to sell. If that's the case, no problem. If you are following The Lifestyle Masterplan™, you've got something great that you can use as your value piece to give away. You may have created that piece with the intention of making money with it, but don't be disappointed. You are using this great content to BUILD your following, which in turn is going to be your most valuable asset!

Products Are Not Assets

One of the biggest problems I see in this industry is that people view the *product* as the asset of the business. It's not. The asset you have is your followers or your list. It is critical to understand that products are a dime a dozen. Name ANY type of information product you can think of, and I'd almost guarantee you can find it for 27 dollars or less online.

Let me provide you with some evidence that products are not an asset. Search the internet for "digital product with resell rights." What you will find are a bunch of information products that can be purchased (usually VERY inexpensively) and that include the

This is one of the biggest things that Multi-Level Marketing companies don't understand. They tell you they are giving you something of value by providing you with a product to sell and they usually will handle the fulfillment. The problem is they don't realize that they've done the easy part (creating a product) and are leaving the hard part up to the person they have recruited with promises of riches.

rights to resell them. You'll see pages and pages of products that you can purchase for literally less than a fast food meal. You wouldn't believe what you can get for 5, 10, 25, 50 bucks. Anyone can go buy these products and resell them. Actually, anyone with an engaged, loyal following can sell them. And they are not all bad products. That's why it is so critical to build that list of loyal and engaged followers. Once you've done that, they'll tell you what they want.

Even if you have a unique, useful, and needed product, you can't do a damn thing with it if you don't have some followers or a list. There are plenty of people who will tell you that you can just post it on social media and it will go viral, or some voodoo like that, but that simply isn't true. Social media IS a solid and effective relationship- and lead-building method, but it's not a panacea; it is one more tool in your box.

As I said, if you did the first two steps well, this one will be easy. It will be easy because you will have already connected with your followers and you are EXTREMELY in touch with what they want and need. Just create it and sell it to them!

Top Off Your Skyscraper

This might be the most exciting part of creating your expert lifestyle business. You have built a following, and now you are ready to find out what they want, then create it and sell it to them. And start making money!

Broadcast Tower Atop the Empire State Building, Courtesy of: Starrcrow13, Wikipedia Commons

But there's more to it than just making money from the products you create. To the right, you'll see a picture of the transmission tower on the Empire State Building. The location and position of this tower atop the Empire State building allows the delivery of broadcasting signals to cable and satellite systems and directly to television and radio receivers reaching over 7.4 million TV households which represent over 6.5% of all TV households in the US. (information courtesy of The Empire State Building's website, esbnyc.com.)

Do you think broadcasters pay big bucks to put their antennas on this tower? You BET! The Empire State Building has the ASSET. They have the ability to reach 7.4 million TV households. That's why they can charge big bucks for broadcasters to use their building to broadcast.

The great news is that by building your following, you are building a broadcast tower that allows you to reach and influence a large number of people. Do you think other marketers will pay to get access to your broadcast tower? Yep. Big time. This is why I keep saying YOUR FOLLOWING is your asset. Not your products.

Now that you have built this broadcast tower, you get to broadcast from it. You get to use that communication medium to find out what your followers want, so you can create it.

I could end the chapter with that — saying 'just create it.' But there is a specific sequence in which you will do this in order to make sure you have success and, most importantly, that you don't waste a bunch of time creating products that people don't buy. So, let's get into that.

Raise Your Spire

The top of your skyscraper is just like the spire that is on the top of most tall structures. The majority of the work is not in putting up the spire, it is in constructing the building. Then, putting the spire on the top is easy. They just raise it up and bolt it on!

It is the same with your expert lifestyle business — most of the work is already done before you actually create products.

Raising your SPIRE takes just five simple steps:

Survey your followers,
Practice with an interactive product,
Integrate what you learned into a hands-off product,
Refine that product, and
Expand your reach with JV partners.

Let's talk about what each of these mean.

Survey Your Followers

In most cases, just by having the dialogue with your followers you are going to get all the information you need to create the first product. But sometimes you can draw out more information with more intentional methods.

EVERY conversation (Facebook message, email, consulting session, seminar, etc.) is an opportunity to learn more about your followers and what they want and need. Treat every interaction that way. You might not get everything you need, or maybe you weren't even thinking about conversations in that manner. Don't worry, it's not too late.

Surveys

You can ask your followers to fill out a survey. In fact, every time someone says no or yes to you, you should ask them why they said no or yes. The amount of intelligence you gather with this is hugely valuable. There are plenty of sites that allow you to create surveys to send out, asking various questions about what your prospects want and need, like and dislike, how much they will pay, etc.

Focus Groups

Focus groups are also a great way to learn more about your niche. This can be an awesome opportunity. Get a small group of folks together to talk — ask them a bunch of questions about what they want or need in a product. In these sessions, you can provide value to them as well, which will make them more likely to want to participate and to provide you with lots of value.

These are just a few of the valuable ways you can get input and feedback from your followers, but they should not replace the individual or group coaching or consulting that we discussed in chapter seven. Individual contact gives you great, intimate interactions with your followers and lets you learn about them on the deepest possible level.

Practice With An Interactive Product

By now you probably have caught on to the fact that I believe that the single most important thing you can do is TALK TO your followers. Talk, talk, talk! This is the only way you can know what they want and need so you can create products and services that will be meaningful to them and that they will want to buy.

At this point, you have done two main things to learn about your followers:

1. You conducted individual or group coaching or consulting, and
2. You created content for them regularly and interacted with them on social media, blog, email and other means.

Now you have gotten to know enough about them to create your first product! Congratulations!

Deliver Your First Product

By this time, you have a pretty good idea of what they want. Now is the time to deliver that to them. And you want to deliver it to them in a way that allows you to continue interacting with them — and heavily at first. You will build this interaction into your first product.

The first product should consist of you teaching something — I guess that's pretty obvious. But it should involve you teaching them directly and having plenty of opportunity to interact in the form of questions, comments, feedback and other back and forth interactions. This could be something like a group coaching program, teleseminar series, or perhaps a live, in-person class or event. The bottom line here is that you are rolling up your sleeves and working WITH your followers to impart knowledge to them. This approach lets you further refine your message. It lets you see exactly what works and what doesn't work when communicating with them. It also helps you learn more about the language they use to describe their problems, issues and desires as they relate to your topic area.

Finally, it gives you a chance to practice teaching. Whether you are experienced as a teacher or not, this practice will be invaluable as you go on to develop more "hands-off" products and services.

The other important thing about your first product is that it should be somewhat "build it as you go." In other words, you're not creating a whole, fully-baked product before selling it. On the other hand, I'm not suggesting that you fly by the seat of your pants either; the idea is that you will adapt this product based on the feedback you get as you go along.

It's A Work-In-Progress
For example, if it were a six week group coaching program (which is a great way to go for your first product), you would have an outline of what you will cover in each of the six weeks — but you won't go to a lot of work preparing week two's content until after week one. Week one will give you some great, valuable insights into what they want, need and find valuable. You will probably get some feedback about the speed of delivery, method of delivery, and will even work through some technical or logistical issues. Then when you develop the content for week two, you will have gathered considerable intelligence to incorporate into your content and delivery mechanism.

Due to the interactivity and direct contact students will have with you, you clearly will want to limit the number of students you allow into a program such as this. You WANT it to be very interactive and very hands-on. You cannot do that well if you have too many students. You probably want to cap this at around 15-20 registrants.

How you do this first product/program will be greatly influenced by how much you have interacted with your followers in the past. For example, if you are a business coach, you may have been talking to people in your niche for many years. Maybe you've even been doing it in a group setting. That's great! That just means you've already done this step or have a really great head start. The important thing is that you get up close and personal with your followers with your first product.

Integrate What You Learned Into A Hands-Off Product

You might want to offer your interactive product a few times before you create the hands-off version. You might offer the hands-off product after six months or perhaps after the first interactive offering ends. What's important is that you only offer the hands-off version when you feel that you have a good understanding of your customers and how to help them.

Are You Frustrated It Took So Long To Get To This Point?

Good – that's intentional! Well, not to frustrate you, but it is intentional to delay this part. This point is highly controversial as it is the single biggest thing that clients, and even some of the big gurus, disagree with me about. The Lifestyle Masterplan™ frustrates people because it takes so long to get to the product part — to get to the hands-off product with profit potential that is. That is very intentional.

How long it takes to get here depends on a number of things. It's completely possible to get to this point in as little as three months, or it could take up to a year. We are talking about LIFESTYLE here and this is the holy grail of lifestyle! I certainly understand the frustration, but remember I'm showing you a way that ACTUALLY WORKS. If you wanted a get-rich-quick book, you would have tossed this in the fireplace six chapters ago, so I'm going to assume you are with me and I won't belabor this point any more.

Packaging What You Know

What happens at this point is that you PACKAGE your knowledge. You are packaging it into something that can be delivered with little or none of your time. In order to create such a hands-off product, you will have to be dialed into what your followers want and need. If you get this product wrong, you've wasted a lot of time. I'd rather you spend that time up front figuring out and tuning into what your followers want, so that your first product is a hit; and you then you can move into creating larger, higher-end products.

The bottom line is this — you are going to spend your time in one of two ways:

1. Getting to know your followers and what they want as outlined here,

OR

2. Creating and re-creating hands-off products because you keep missing the mark.

I created my first product way before I knew enough about how my followers defined their problem or what they really needed. That first product offered great material and it was a quality product (if you don't measure the quality of a product by the number of people who buy it!). The problem was that it simply didn't address the RIGHT problem for my followers. That's why they didn't buy it. But were it not for that mistake (and many more like it), I wouldn't have developed this powerful system.

Golden Intellectual Capital

Once you have created and offered your interactive program for the first time, you are going to have a BUNCH of feedback and "intellectual capital" about your offering, your followers, what works, what doesn't work, etc. This is golden information that you will use as you create your hands-off product. You have now learned much more about how to talk to your followers, as well as what they want and need on a much deeper level. You've also seen some of what works and what doesn't work for them. Now is the time to dive deeper and create something that can be sold and delivered with less (but probably not none) of your time.

This is where you are trying to get to! This is where you begin to create that revenue stream that will give you the freedom you are reading this book for.

Choosing A Delivery Format
There are a lot of ways that you can format this product, which I call your flagship product. The most common way to do this is to create a series of video training modules. You can put these video training modules on a membership site. They can also be delivered over the phone as a teleseminar series, or via any number of other ways. There are pros and cons to each delivery method, but the most important factor is how your followers want it to be delivered. Just ask them, you've created the connection already.

Your product can also be delivered in the form of audio, DVD, workbook, or another physical media. Don't be intimidated by the idea of having something physically created and shipped. It is VERY easy these days. I'm not saying that shipping a physical product is right or appropriate for everyone, but in many cases, it may be something that will differentiate you or add considerable value in your customers' eyes.

Launch Your Flagship Product To Your Followers

We talked in chapter seven about how important it is to build relationships with other people in your area of knowledge so that you can get access to their audience. This will happen slowly at first. It will start with you working with people who are your size and smaller; soon you'll be connecting with people who are slightly bigger than you, and it will snowball from there. Because these relationships are so extremely important, you don't want to screw them up! That is exactly why you will launch your products to your own followers (your email list) FIRST, before you launch them with your JV partners. If you launched a product with your JV partners and it missed the mark (i.e. it didn't sell well or you had issues delivering it), you could damage these very important relationships that you spent so much time cultivating.

Work Out The Kinks

Now that you have your product created, you are all set to launch it to your own followers. You have the product, but just like everything, it's not perfect yet! You are going to continue to get feedback on how it can be better as long as you are offering it, but you'll want to get the first round of feedback from your own folks (who you are closest to, trust you, and with whom you have the strongest relationship). Then you'll incorporate that feedback before you go on to launch it with your JV partners.

Launching a product to your own list is also the SIMPLEST way to get rolling. The basic way to launch a product is to email a series of about three engaging, value-packed videos to them, then a fourth video that offers the product for sale.

Generally, the videos are spaced as follows:

> *Day 1:*   Video 1
> *Day 4:*   Video 2
> *Day 7:*   Video 3
> *Day 10:* Video 4; shopping cart opens (product is available for sale)
> *Day 14:* Shopping cart closes (product is no longer for sale)

The days listed above are the major releases of new video. The days in between are great opportunities to insert additional content, follow-ups and reminders to your list. In other words, on day two you might send an email follow-up to remind your followers to watch the video and, of course, be sure to couple that with some content or information that will be beneficial to them.

Expand Your Reach With JV Partners

Once you've executed that first launch and worked out the kinks, you'll be ready to start working with your JV (Joint Venture) partners to launch your product. That's where you are going to see a lot of growth in your list and your business. Just remember that this is a LOT of work! It requires a ton of coordination. None of it is hard; it just needs to be very well coordinated and managed.

Evergreen Launches (Make Money While You Sleep)

I hate the phrase "make money while you sleep." So often it is used to lure people into some type of internet marketing or multi-level marketing voodoo. If you google "make money while you sleep," you will get all kinds of silly information and promises about making money while you sleep. When I worked in the corporate world, I made money while I slept as well. The paycheck was deposited in my account every other Friday at midnight while I slept, but in order to earn that money, I gave up 80 hours of my life every two weeks. That's not what we're talking about here!

I'll never forget the first time I had an order come in from an online promotion. It was on a Saturday afternoon and I had the flu. I was really sick and had been confined to bed all day. Finally, I got up enough energy to check my email. In my inbox was an order! I was so excited because it was the first time I had truly "made money while I slept." After that, I got to thinking about how cool it was.

I'm not trying to be a downer. I do want to illustrate that the work is on the front end in order to earn those sales. After that, when the cash really does start rolling in "while you sleep," it is a tremendous feeling. You are building something amazing here and I don't want to take away from that. I do, however, want to be the guy who is real with you about it. It IS hard work. And it is totally worth it.

Automating Your Income Stream

The ultimate way to make money is to have it automated. You'll set up your flagship product with an automated launch sequence. That means that people will come to your web site or squeeze page and enter their email address. Then they will get a series of videos that teach about your area of expertise, and then they'll receive a fourth and final video that offers your product for sale.

Of course, this series of videos and emails is sent automatically through your email provider. I'm not suggesting you send these manually — that would not be a lifestyle business!

Just like when you launched to your followers, the product must cease to be available at the end of the launch. This ensures buyers are motivated to purchase now, and doesn't allow for the natural human desire to wait for an indefinite period of time.

This can become the bread and butter of your business. Once you get this process working well, you will have regular passive income — which is pretty awesome. The key here is: "once you get it working well." Again, this is definitely something you can do, but it's not a "slap it up and they will buy" type of thing. You will have to work with the content and look closely at how it's going, and continue to tweak it as you go.

Give Them More!

If you are giving your followers great value in your products (and I know you are or you wouldn't be reading this), then at least some of them are going to want more. For example, if they go through your interactive program, you will have people who want one-on-one consulting or coaching. If they purchase your flagship product, some will want to be involved in a more interactive experience. Some will go through your products and then want more depth in a certain area. You must serve those people! If you don't, you are leaving money on the table; and more importantly, you aren't giving them what they really want and need.

What's The Next Step?

It's important to have a "next step" for everyone. For example, in a group program, you might toss in an extra session or something like that, to provide a little more value AND introduce another way to go farther with you.

> Caution: Don't use time during a program they have paid for as an opportunity to sell them. Remember, you always want to deliver tremendous value. Then you'll find they naturally want more (and then you can offer them something else to buy.) Do you sales pitch outside of the paid time.

One of the basic principles of business is that it is cheaper and easier to sell to an existing customer than to acquire a new one, so always have something to offer existing customers after they complete your program or product. If you don't have anything, you can always offer other people's products and services to your list as an affiliate or joint venture.

This whole process keeps on going as long as you have a business. You will continuously create new products and programs and refine them, dropping old products and creating new ones. The point you want to get to is where you have a wide selection of products that appeal to people on different parts of their journey and at different price points. This is when you will become very profitable with your business.

It's All About Getting A Customer

The only asset even more valuable than your followers is your customers. Your flagship product will make you money, but that's not the biggest benefit that it has. Its biggest benefit is that it has created a customer. Once you have a customer, you get the opportunity to WOW them. You get to deliver amazing value to them, so they will want MORE. Yes, more! This is when it gets really crazy awesome.

Each time you create and sell a product, you must look at it from the standpoint of what you are going to sell them next. I never sell a product without knowing what I will sell to that customer NEXT. If they buy a $197 product, there is something next. At the conclusion of that product or program, there will be another product for sale.

Conclusion

This is the easiest part of The Lifestyle Masterplan™. But it's only easy if you do the previous steps. So cement your foundation and erect your structure first (and do it well), and then this part will be a cake walk.

Think Of It Like This:

- ✗ The better you know your prospects (by talking to them), the better products you will be able to create for them AND the more likely they will be to buy from you.
- ✗ When they buy from you, that's a golden opportunity to learn what worked and didn't work in that product, and what they want next.
- ✗ Just get the customers. I don't care if you get them at a 20 dollar or 5000 dollar price point, the most important thing is that you get them. Then you can wow the heck out of them so they keep buying.

Do It Like This:

- ✓ Create a high-touch, hands-on product to learn more about your followers and how to deliver information to them.
- ✓ Create your flagship hands-off product based on what you learned from that first product.
- ✓ Set your flagship product on autopilot with an evergreen launch.
- ✓ Create "next step" higher-end products to sell to your customers.

Chapter 9

Make Technology Work For You

"We've arranged a civilization in which most crucial elements profoundly depend on science and technology."
— Carl Sagan

I'm really opinionated about technology for a few reasons, but mainly because of the ridiculous amount of experience I have working with it. I've been the guy who sets up and fixes your computer, the guy who manages multi-million dollar website conversions and everything in between. So I know a few things.

Managing large technology initiatives for 15 years gave me a great deal of knowledge about how to use software to enable a business to operate as efficiently and on as large a scale as possible. That experience gave me about 1000% of the knowledge I need to handle the software for an expert lifestyle business. In other words, I really only use about 10% of my knowledge in my expert lifestyle business and I'm giving you that 10% here. My challenge in writing this chapter is to pare down what I know into ONLY what you need to know.

Now when I say I know a few things, I'm not necessarily talking about nuts and bolts or detailed technical knowledge. I have some of that, but I don't make an effort to keep up with the rapid change that occurs in technology. That's what my technical team is for.

What I do know is how to make it work FOR me.

Clients say to me all the time, "But I don't understand technology."

MY RESPONSE: "You don't need to."

This is 2013. While you do not need to understand technology, you DO need to understand how to manage technology.

Don't expect me to start talking about bits and bytes and configuring this and that. I don't do that stuff and you shouldn't either. I'm giving you the right way to think about technology, which is essential to creating your expert lifestyle business.

Your Technology Mindset

Like most things in life, mastering technology is about MINDSET.

The most important thing to remember with regard to technology is that it is YOUR tool. YOU own it. YOU control it. YOU tell it what to do.

Many people, particularly those about 40+, think of it the other way around. They view technology as something that was done TO THEM rather than something that is FOR THEM. This is a crippling mentality.

It's just like an auto mechanic. His air-powered wrench is not something that was thrust upon him against his will. His air-powered wrench is something he views as a great tool that lets him loosen bolts with just a pull of the trigger and very little muscle. This is in contrast to his grandfather who didn't have that tool at his disposal. His grandfather had to use a lot more muscle to break that same bolt.

Technology is YOUR tool. You control it. You don't need to understand it and you don't need to know HOW it works. You just need to be in charge of it and you must think that way. This is pure mindset. I'm going to give you all the practical knowledge you need.

A Confession

Now for a confession: I'm nearly 40 years old as I write this. I have a unique advantage, or perspective, that allows me to see multiple viewpoints. People my age are what I call "tech tweeners."

The thing about this particular age is that I am old enough to remember the days before the internet and technology became as prevalent as they are today, BUT I'm still young enough to embrace them.

I know how to use a computer. I know how to do almost anything, and if I don't, I know how to figure it out. However, I also have the perspective of older folks who are less savvy, in that I struggle with the whole mobile thing. I don't like smartphones. A tiny little computer that doesn't have a keyboard doesn't sound very smart to me. I want a full-sized computer. Younger people do almost everything on their smartphone! Which to me is insane. So I'm seeing it from both sides.

However, I do *understand* the mobile world. I understand the importance of it and the necessity to be compatible with mobile. You'll see the QR codes throughout this book. I include them to enable those who are mobile savvy to get more information as they read along. If I were reading this book, I probably wouldn't use the QR codes, but they are there because the book wasn't written for me, it was written for YOU! If you don't want to get more information on your mobile phone, I've included URLs so you can go get it on your big-boy or big-girl computer, instead of your "smart" phone, which is what I would do!

It's Just Like Owning A Car

Since my background gives me such a great advantage in terms of technology, I find it useful to compare the struggles that other people have with technology to how I manage my vehicle. I am completely "CAR illiterate," meaning I have very little understanding of how an internal combustion engine works. I know that you put gas and a key in it and it goes. If it won't start, I know to first check if it has gas. If it has gas and the key is in it, then I'm out of ideas as to why it's not starting. I need help!

But if I didn't have a car, I'd be in a world of hurt because I am dependent on that vehicle. Does it make me uncomfortable that I don't know how it works? No, that's why I have AAA and a great mechanic.

Likewise, you need the equivalent of AAA and a great mechanic to manage the technology in your expert business.

Mastering Technology

Once you've changed your mindset about technology, in order to master technology you will need to remember four key things:

1. Don't confuse marketing with technology.
2. You can't afford FREE.
3. Consider everyone's perspective.
4. Be clear about your goals.

1. Don't Confuse Marketing With Technology

It's important that you don't let technology people make your marketing decisions! Unfortunately, this happens all the time.

At the end of the day, as experts, we are direct marketers of information. My primary business is marketing. My strongest skill is and always will be marketing.

> This is rule #1 in my business:
> *Nobody but me makes marketing decisions.*

I frequently seek the counsel of others on matters related to marketing, but when it comes to the final decision, the buck stops with me. If I do seek marketing advice from others, it is because they have knowledge about marketing — usually that means they have a valuable perspective that complements mine or they have skills and experience that I don't have.

These days, we use technology A LOT in marketing. That's the world we live in. But marketers are marketers, and technologists are technologists, and both need to stay on their side of the playground.

Marketing and technology are two topics that intimidate many people. What typically happens is that well-meaning technologists tout the marketing benefits of the technology or technology solutions they are selling.

That really scares me.

Find The Right Expert For The Job

People who haven't worked in technology usually don't realize how many diverse and segmented skill sets exist within the technology world. A perfect example of this is design and development. Designing a website or software and actually creating it are two entirely different skill sets. In fact, it requires two different sides of the brain! It is just like building a house.

Have you EVER seen an architect swing a hammer? Have you ever seen a drywaller at a drafting table? No. It's the same with the field of technology.

Let's say you are building a house. What would you think if your builder said, "I can do it all. I don't need an architect. I know how to design your house; I can do the plumbing, drywall and even lay the carpet."? You would kick them out on their butt! The same goes for having a website created. Never leave designing the website to the "builder." They are separate skill sets with separate knowledge and experience required and should be done by individuals with the appropriate experience and knowledge.

The exception to this is web development companies or agencies that have both types of experts in-house. That is perfectly fine and I highly recommend working with such an organization. When you work with them, you will have both skill sets available, as well as an account manager whose job it is to communicate with you and coordinate between you and the various experts within the agency. We'll talk more about this later in this chapter.

Hint: It's Not Your Nephew!
Please don't hire your nephew because he's "good with the computer." If it were possible, I would get down on my hands and knees and plead with you on this one!

I'm sure your 16-year-old nephew is a great kid, gets good grades, is honest, smart, and has a very bright future ahead of him. I'm not knocking him as a person. He's probably also good with technology and can do just about anything from social media to websites to fixing your iPhone.

But please don't hire him to do your social media or technology.

The fact that he is young, probably cheap, and tech-savvy is appealing. I get that. But he's not a marketer. Posting pictures and regular statuses on Facebook, tweeting about his favorite sports team, and checking in every place he goes demonstrate his understanding of how to use the technology in the context of his life as a 16-year-old kid. However, it does not indicate an understanding of how to actually *market* your expert business.

The point here is to understand the skill sets that each person brings to the table. An understanding and willingness to use technology is a commodity skill. Actually knowing how to market the business is a whole different story and requires a specific marketing skill set.

> DISCLAIMER: If your 16-year-old nephew is a brilliant and experienced marketer, please strike everything I said above and hire him immediately, and send him a tweet with my apologies.

2. You Can't Afford Free

There are a lot of "free" services out there — free email, free websites, free webinar software, etc. Pretty much anything you can imagine you can get for free. Sometimes the free version is limited in what you can do with it. Sometimes it means you have to look at advertisements. Either way, it means that you are NOT in control.

When you use free services, the company you are working with owes you absolutely NOTHING. Compare it to your business — what value do you give to a paying customer vs. someone who comes to your website and consumes content you provide for free? Certainly you value your website visitors and feel a sense of responsibility to them, but when the rubber meets the road, who will receive more of your limited time and resources: the people who pay you or the people who don't?

Your online resources are critical to your business and need to be provided by someone who has "skin in the game" — someone who is taking your money and in return has a responsibility and an incentive to keep you happy so they can keep receiving your money.

This is a lesson that comes directly from my experience in the corporate world where software failure could result in tens or hundreds of thousands of dollars per minute in losses. While you probably don't have *that* much at stake, the point remains that your technology providers need to be partners, and your resource providers must have something at stake. The best way to get technology partners to have something at stake is to pay them. This gives you the ability to *stop* paying them (fire them) if you are unhappy with the service they provide.

When people excitedly say, "There's a FREE <whatever> at www.somefreecrap.com," don't get excited. Instead, cringe and run the other way. Your technology is a key part of your business and you can't afford *free*.

3. Consider Everyone's Perspective

You have to realize where people (namely people trying to sell you something) are coming from. What is their objective? What are THEY trying to accomplish?

Let's take, for example, the "app guy." I'll call him the app guy because he sells apps. When I say app, I'm referring to the applications we install on our phones. These apps provide some sort of information or functionality. (I'm not talking about the mozzarella sticks you get at TGIFriday's!)

The app guy tells you the fantastic and amazing benefits of having an app for your business. He tells you that you *need* to have an app because people will download it and put it on their phone, and your business will be with them all the time. He tells you how much money people have made from apps, how quickly people have grown their lists, and that simply EVERYONE has an app; and if you don't, you might as well ride a dinosaur.

Let's take a moment to look at his perspective and motivation.

He is trying to sell you an app. Or a book about apps. Or training on apps. It doesn't matter — the point is that he is biased when it comes to apps. I'm not suggesting he is dishonest, misleading, wrong, or anything like that. I am saying that he has a vested interest in getting you to believe that you need an app.

By the way, you probably don't need an app. In order for an app to be beneficial, it's likely going to cost more than it's worth. If you see an offer for an app that is cheap — there is a reason it is cheap, and you won't receive any more benefit from it than you pay for it.

Does It Fit My Strategy?

You must be able to stand back and look at your entire strategy for getting known and building this business; then consider how that app fits into your overall strategic picture. If you are reading this book, you're going to have that overall picture by the time you finish reading, so good for you!

The point is that you have to be the master of your destiny, which means having a solid strategy for building your business. That means not looking to the app guy to solve your problems with a bunch of promises about how this app is going to send you a ton of leads or sales.

Companies selling software also frequently tout the features of their software, websites or services. The software industry is very "feature-centric," meaning that software is sold, compared and evaluated on its features. Features are the things that software does, such as social media integration, tracking and statistics or other automatic functions.

Because software companies live and die based on their features and how successfully they can sell them, they will pump up the value of these features to a level that is sometimes ridiculous. My personal favorite is social media integration. Don't be lured by the hype and false promises made by software companies about their social media integration. Social media needs to be planned and managed deliberately, not in the way that each and every software company has decided to integrate it into their software tool.

The Tools Won't Do It For You

Here is a great way to look at software and other technology tools within the framework of your expert lifestyle business. Think of yourself as a carpenter. As a carpenter, you must know how to ACTUALLY DO carpentry! Right? Of course! You have to know how to pound a nail, cut a board to 87 inches long and make a mitre cut at 47 degrees when the plans call for it. Carpenters also have lots of great tools that make their job easier. In fact, carpenters couldn't do most of their work without tools. I'm not aware of a way to make a mitre cut without some sort of tool.

If you were to hire a carpenter to build a bookshelf, you would make sure that carpenter really KNOWS how to do carpentry. Would you hire a carpenter who said, "I've never really built anything before, but I have ALL the best tools."? No way! You would send him packing.

Think of your software tools in exactly the same way — they will not "do for you" or "make possible" anything you don't already know how to do. You have to know how to do the marketing and promotion of your business FIRST, and then you can find and use the tools that will make your job easier. The good news is that you are reading this book, so that means you are well on your way to knowing EXACTLY how to market your expert business!

The Pros And Cons Of Software

If you are investing in software or a tool that you believe is going to do for you what you believe you cannot do, you are wasting your money. You are throwing money at a problem. That never works. In general, software doesn't solve problems; it automates processes. You have to know what you are automating with the software.

When you approach your software tools with this perspective, you can use software to do some amazing things! You will be able to use software (as well as outsourcing) to get a whole lot of work done with a very small amount of effort and (most importantly) less of YOUR valuable time.

4. Be Clear About Your Goals

This is the most important one to remember. YOU ARE THE BOSS! YOU make the decisions. YOU set the direction of your business. This is why it is so important to have a strategy.

A trap that I see experts fall into frequently is one of getting confused or frustrated and letting the wrong people make decisions for them. For example, not knowing what should be on your website and letting a website developer make that decision for you.

Being clear about your goals is especially important when it comes to using technology to promote your business. Too often we get caught in the "technology for the sake of technology" trap. The "gottahaveanapp" syndrome that we just talked about is a perfect example of that.

Being crystal clear on what you are trying to accomplish with your website, social media, app, membership site, or whatever it may be, eliminates a bunch of problems and issues right up front. When you know what you want to accomplish, it is simpler.

When the word *cool* is used to describe virtually anything technology-related, it generally means we are looking at it from the wrong perspective. Be clear about your goals and everything will be "cool."

The Key Question To Ask

When you find yourself in a technology-based situation, start by asking yourself this simple question: "What am I trying to accomplish right now?"

If you are having a website created, you probably have one primary goal: to collect leads. That's pretty much what we use websites for these days. Each and every time someone comes to your website, it should be doing one thing: collecting the lead! That clear goal will then drive every decision you make about your website creation. The wonderful thing about being this clear and focused is that when a web developer you are working with tells you that you MUST have a flash presentation on your website because it is so cool, you know what to ask him:

"Will that enhance my ability to collect leads?"

More About Your Website

Ongoing Maintenance

This is easy to forget. We get a website up and running and think "Yay! We're done!" Unfortunately, technology is just like your car. When you first buy your car, get your tags and insurance, you are all set — for a while! Then comes the first oil change, brakes wear out, tires need to be replaced and, of course, there will be unexpected breakdowns.

Your technology is EXACTLY the same way. You will need to have security patches and upgrades installed on a regular basis. And, yes, unfortunately, you are going to have dreaded breakdowns! There will be problems with your hosting provider, security issues and people will make mistakes that will bring your site down or create issues. It's just a fact of life. That is exactly why you need to have the technology TEAM that we're going to discuss later. It's less important HOW you ensure these things are done, than it is that you are certain that they ARE done.

Updatability

Your business will change. You will develop new products, create new content and all sorts of other things will come up that will cause you to want to add to or edit content on your website.

You will need to be able to put information and revisions out there quickly!

For example, just the other day I was being interviewed and the host asked me where his listeners could go to get a specific piece of information. I knew it wasn't on my website! Being the quick thinker that I am, I quickly rattled off a URL (that didn't exist yet) that they could go to. Once the interview was finished, I quickly set that page up. That worked out okay because I have a mechanism to get new content onto my website within minutes.

Recognize that you have to be able to make updates quickly and regularly to your website. It doesn't matter if you have it designed so you can do it yourself, or if you have someone on speed dial who can do it for you, as long as you can get it out there quickly.

> DISCLAIMER: I don't believe that we, as experts, are "Internet Marketers." I don't even believe this is an "Internet Business." I don't think that what we are doing here is "about" technology. It is about *information*.

Technology Team

With that said, I have to add that an expert lifestyle business IS hugely dependent upon technology. Technology is an important, in fact critical, part of our businesses. And that is why we need a technology team. Fortunately for you, a technology team does not mean a three-story building with 150 tech people! It can mean just a few relationships with key people who know you and your business.

Your technology is DAMN important for your expert lifestyle business.

Website Down = Business Down

If your website goes down, your ability to collect leads and sell are down also. It's not that your website is down – it's that your business is down. For that reason, you simply must have "go to" people.

If your business is down, you don't have time to:

1. Find a Wordpress expert (or whatever expert is needed),
2. Check his/her references,
3. Provide him/her with the login information for your servers,
4. Familiarize him/her with your business,
5. Explain the problem and how you would like it solved,
6. Manage him/her to completion of the issue,
7. Validate completion of the issue, and
8. Pay him/her.

What you need is to have that expert resource on speed dial. I highly recommend using a third-party service such as eLance or Odesk as a tool to manage the logistics of these relationships. Those services will provide you with a robust set of tools to manage payments, supervision, reviews by your peers, etc. However, none of that is a replacement for a good, solid understanding of how to select and manage employees. We'll talk more about this in chapter 10.

You also need to take your lifestyle into consideration. I recently had my main website go down late on Christmas Eve! Since I had planned to be away from my business at that time, I was glad that I had a support system in place to ensure this could be handled with only a small amount of my time and effort.

Building these relationships with technology people on "speed dial" isn't hard. The best way to do it is to look at each interaction with a technologist as an opportunity to build your team. If you are working with a company or individual to develop your website, look at it with an eye towards making that a long-term relationship. Is this someone you want to continue working with? Is this someone who has the skills and abilities that you need?

Agency Versus Individuals

There are two types of technologists you can work with: agencies or individuals.

Agency: Agencies are companies that have assembled a team of people who are there to meet your needs. They MAY (not always) have marketing and technology staff in-house. I believe this is the BEST option for experts who are serious about building an expert lifestyle business. As I said earlier, we cannot let technology people make marketing decisions or give us marketing advice. That is why I love the agency model —both sets of expertise are available in-house. You should absolutely use this model if it is feasible. You will have a marketing person to shepherd you through how your strategy can be automated and enhanced by technology. This person understands marketing AND knows how to communicate your needs to the technical staff.

The downside to the agency model is cost. It will be considerably more expensive than working with individual contractors. And I realize it may not be feasible in all situations, so let's talk about working with individual contractors.

Individual: In this case, you will seek out individual contractors to work with by using Odesk, elance, private contracts, or other services. We'll talk more about hiring contractors in chapter 10. but the bottom line is that you are taking on the task of managing and controlling these contractors. Since YOU are in charge, you must be clear about what your goals are, what you want this technology to accomplish and you must make sure that the contractor is doing what you have asked and that everything is functioning as you expect. Make sure you have intermediate checkpoints built into the process so you can see how things are progressing along the way. You don't want to get to the end of the project and be disappointed with the result.

The downside of hiring contractors directly is that you have to be more clear and more involved in the whole process than you would be with an agency. However, it will definitely cost less.

Technology Resources

I want to provide a comprehensive list of the technologies you need for your expert lifestyle business, and because these things change so fast, I put the list online so I can update it regularly. For the list, please visit:

howtoquitworkingbook.com/technology

Conclusion

If I could sum up this entire chapter in one sentence, it would be:

YOU are the master of technology in your business.

Technology is there for one reason only, and that is to enable your business to run as efficiently and on as large of a scale as possible.

Embrace it; love it; make it do your bidding.

Think Of It Like This:

- ✘ YOU are in charge of the technology in your business; technologists are implementers who make YOUR vision happen.
- ✘ Your business depends on technology. That doesn't mean you have to understand it; but you do have to understand how to get it done.
- ✘ You can't afford FREE.
- ✘ Technology and marketing are TOTALLY different disciplines. Technology decisions are made by technology experts and marketing decisions are made by marketing experts.

Do It Like This:

- ✓ Build relationships with technology people or agencies so you can get the support you need when you need it.
- ✓ Clearly understand and document your goals and what you expect to get out of a piece of technology BEFORE you begin working with a technologist to create it.
- ✓ Be conscious of the updatability and ongoing maintenance that are required for every piece of technology you implement.

Chapter 10

People And Processes

> *"The system is that there is no system. That doesn't mean we don't have process. Apple is a very disciplined company and we have great processes. But that's not what it's about. Process makes you more efficient."*
> - Steve Jobs

Much of the way I approach building an expert lifestyle business (and life in general) is based on one simple concept:

"Your time is the most precious resource you possess."

Nothing makes me more insane than when people say, "It's just time." or "If you don't have time, make time." or my personal favorite, "That will only take x". It doesn't matter if "x" is five minutes, an hour or an entire day; it's still a load of crap.

Is it possible to get more money? Yes.

Is it possible to get more help? Yes.

Is it possible to get more resources? Yes.

Is it possible to get more time? Never.

Running an expert lifestyle business is very different from running a restaurant or other traditional business. The business is about YOU, the expert. That means YOU have to be a part of everything. Your personality, your face, your knowledge, your methods and techniques are the centerpiece of the business. These are what make you different from anyone else out there.

You are also doing this because you want freedom in your life. But how can you have freedom if you are the centerpiece of your business; if YOU are the glue that holds everything together; if YOU are the thing that makes your business different, and therefore viable?

Processes: How To Leverage Yourself

The answer is you do it by leveraging yourself — an absolutely critical aspect of this business. Let me give you an example.

Example: My Lead Process

When a new lead comes into my business, the most effective way for me to convert them into a paying customer is to engage with them personally. How would I do that? Give them a phone call? Send them an email? Give them a complimentary consulting session? Send them a free report? Mail them a hard copy of that report? Sure, those are all great things to do, but there has to be a process for it. Let's break down that process:

The Time-Consuming Lead Process
A new lead comes into your business:
1. Gather their information and do research to learn more about them (very easy, thanks to the internet, but still time-consuming): 30 minutes minimum
2. Compose an email to them: 25 minutes
3. Give them a courtesy phone call: 20 minutes
4. Mail (snail mail) them a free report or piece of content: 10 minutes

This totals 85 minutes. That is nearly an hour and a half. If we do that for 10 leads a week, that's 850 minutes; which is 14 hours. We haven't even done anything meaningful, like offer a complimentary session yet!

What if we could leverage our time better? Let's look at this a little differently.

The Leveraged Lead Process
A new lead comes into your business:
1. You enter them (just bare bones information) into your Customer Relationship Management (CRM) System: 2 minutes
2. You have an assistant who researches this person, gathers their contact information, website, phone numbers, etc., giving you a fairly complete picture of who that person is and what is publicly available about them.
3. An introductory (pre-written) email is composed and sent, either by your assistant or if you are really a fancy-pants, automatically by your CRM system. This email is pre-written generically, but can be customized by inserting fields from your CRM, or manually by your assistant.

4. Give them a courtesy phone call. Maybe this makes sense in your case, maybe not. If your assistant can't find a phone number, obviously you can't do this. But here is the cool thing. Your assistant or your CRM system NOTIFIES you that you have someone to call, but ONLY if a phone number exists. If a phone number doesn't exist, you are not bothered with this step. If this happens, let's say it takes: 20 minutes.

5. Send a snail mail piece to this person. Maybe it's a letter or a report of some sort (probably both); it doesn't matter. The important thing is that it invites them to do something — call you, visit your website, or something else.

How much time did this take you? 25 minutes at the most. And if there was no phone number to be found, it was only five minutes.

Higher-Touch Engagement

Next, if they have responded and shown interest in what you are saying, you will want to get them into a "higher-touch" (as they say in the marketing world) engagement. This will vary by your area of expertise. I use complimentary consulting sessions very effectively. As my business grows, I'm getting more and more selective about whom I will give complimentary sessions to. If you are a coach, this may be a complimentary coaching session, mini-session, etc.

When I provide these, they take a minimum of two hours. Even if the session is one hour, logistics, prep, follow-up and wrap-up are easily another hour of time. Initially, I did a dual session which was two one-hour sessions. While this was incredibly valuable, I've moved away from these because they are too time-consuming. I don't regret doing them. They were extremely valuable at the time, but no longer are they the most effective use of my time. This is all a part of how your business evolves over time.

Systems Are Awesome

Now I've shown you how to do one of the most time-consuming parts of building your business in the least time-consuming manner! The lead follow-up system I outlined is awesome. It's also fairly simple. Start simple, and grow your systems as you can. Make it more and more fancy, elaborate and effective as you master it. Invest a lot of time in building this because you will get massive dividends from it.

Think Of Your Business System And Processes Like A Train

They are the train I built to do all the repetitive tasks of my business. I built the train, put fuel in it, and it goes. It just goes and goes and goes, pulling my business along with it. The cars you attach to the train are business processes. You can hook as many on as you want. Once you have the train, it's easy to just hitch another car onto the end! Of course, like anything else, you will need more power for your train eventually. That's ok; you can just add another locomotive.

This is one of the most powerful parts of building an expert lifestyle business (or any business!). When your systems are set up and running, you can focus on the higher-value activities and utilize your time much more efficiently. Higher-value activities are things like delivering live speeches or presentations, giving complimentary sessions, consulting, creating content, building products and programs and all that stuff that is actually WHY you got into this business in the first place! Or, you can do something completely unrelated to your business. We are building a LIFESTYLE here!

Building The Train: Creating Your Business Processes

How do you build the train? It's pretty easy. I built lots of business processes in my corporate career. I'll give you a quick overview here.

The Process Mindset

There are two things you have to keep in mind while creating your business processes:

1. YOU don't have to do everything. Be ruthless about what you take off your plate. If you think you HAVE to do something yourself, really challenge that. Is it TRULY something that only YOU can do? Or could you provide detailed instructions to someone else to do it?
2. No task is so small it can't be systematized. Don't fall into the trap of saying, "That only takes five minutes, I'll just do it myself." That's a business-killer. Those five minutes will add up. You'll "five minutes" yourself to insanity!

How To Break It Down

The way to break activities down into systems is to look at them on a very detailed level. What are the individual components that make up a task or activity? Each one of those very-detailed items should be examined to identify the lowest possible skill set required to accomplish that task. Is it so straightforward that an assistant could do it? Does it require a copywriter? Does it require a technical person? All tasks must be broken down to their lowest possible level and clearly documented.

Write It Down

Next, document the detail of each task for each person involved. EVEN YOU! Write out step-by-step what each person does, when they do it, and how they do it. There is no such thing as too much detail here. Everyone must know what they do and to a small degree be aware of what others are doing. Each person involved in the process (in a small expert lifestyle business, this is most likely three or fewer people), must know exactly what they need to do, down to the lowest level of detail.

The best way to do this is to literally write it like you are writing it for a 6th grader. It should be on that level of detail. Don't worry about insulting someone's intelligence. When working with processes, the devil is definitely in the details, and assumptions will result in mistakes and ineffectiveness.

Don't Forget The Handoffs

You also must document the handoffs. For example, if you have a blogging process and you write and email the post to your assistant to spell-check and publish it, then your assistant needs to know that their part of the process starts when they receive an email from you with a blog post.

The beauty of this is that once you hit send on the email, you are done. Your assistant takes it from there. Maybe he or she subsequently hands it off to someone else, but that's their job, not yours. You've created your content and now you are back to doing what you enjoy and what gets you excited. Business is still happening while you are eating dinner, sleeping or having a glass of wine!

Work While You Sleep

A lot of the internet marketing gurus talk about making money "while you sleep." I definitely see the appeal of that. What gets me even more excited though is when work is getting done while I sleep!

That was a fast and simple summary of how to build business processes, but you've got the idea. It's not hard to do, but does require you to look at things at a lower level of detail and in a slightly different way than you normally would. Getting that train rolling is what will get your expert lifestyle business rolling, so don't take this step lightly.

People: Staffing

I learned a tremendous amount about selecting, hiring and working with staff during my 15 years in the corporate world. This is another one of those great situations where I actually know a lot more than I need to know to run an expert lifestyle business. That's great for you, because that means I can give you all you need right here!

Independent Contractors

First, when I say hire someone; I'm not talking about a traditional employee. I'm referring to an independent contractor. In the US, this is the difference between a W-2 employee and a 1099 contractor. That is how the US tax code defines them, but the difference is that you have to pay certain taxes and come under a lot of additional regulation if you have an actual employee. I won't get into all the details, but in general, you will want your first few workers to be independent contractors.

Where To Find Them

I highly recommend using one of the major online services that are meant to connect workers with people who need work. A few examples are Odesk and eLance. I primarily use Odesk. I don't necessarily recommend one over the other. There are several others, but as of now, those are the major ones.

These services provide an infrastructure that enables you to connect with, hire, manage and pay independent contractors. They handle the logistics of paying the contractor; so for you, the only thing you have to do is keep a credit card on file with them. They take a fee of around 10%, which is more than worth it.

The other great thing that these services offer is the ability to monitor the contractor's work. If it is an hourly job, Odesk actually takes screen shots of the contractor's computer screen so that you can see what they have been working on. That's a really cool feature and can be useful. However, if you need to spend a lot of time evaluating those screen captures, then you hired the wrong person. This is a great time to talk about how to actually make that selection.

How To Hire A Contractor

Selecting a contractor is a three-step process:

1. Define what you need in a contractor.
2. Select and hire the contractor.
3. Monitor and manage the work.

Define What You Need In A Contractor

Before you try to select someone, you must figure out what it is that you need. Think in terms of the skills they must possess, as well as how much time it will take to do the job, how long you will need them, and very specifically, what tasks they will do.

Think about what the person needs to have in terms of skills. Do they need to know how to use Excel and Word? Do they need technical skills? Get clear on the skills they need to have *before* you think about hiring someone.

Consider whether you are able to use contractors who are not from your native country. There are a lot of advantages to using offshore contractors. They can be considerably cheaper and may bring fresh perspectives to your situation. However, they may not speak English as their first language. This is OK in many situations; but many tasks will require English as a first language. I don't use non-native English speakers for anything that involves creating written content. I want all the words to be from me or a native English speaker. Customer support is perfectly fine to be done by someone whose first language is not English, as long as their English is good enough to be easily understood.

Select And 'Hire' The Contractor

I put 'hire' in quotes because I want to be clear that this is not a traditional *hiring* situation. There are a few things to remember here. Since you know what you need (you already defined that earlier in this chapter), the first step is to weed out everyone who *doesn't have* those skills or attributes. That will get it down to a much smaller list.

Check Their Reviews And Work History

Sites like Odesk and eLance have great review functions where you can see exactly what other employers have said about each contractor. Sometimes you can see the actual job description of what the contractor did for the reviewer. That can be very helpful. Make sure you look at the employer reviews carefully. If there are none or if the contractor has not done any work on that site yet, just move on. You want someone with a proven track record.

Interview Them

As with any hiring situation, you should request references from other people who have seen their work. You should also do an interview with the contractor either over Skype or the phone to get a better idea of what they are like and how they communicate. After all that, you have to trust your gut or your intuition. That is the most important tool you have in this process.

I'll give you an awesome little tip I picked up about using Odesk and other sites like it. Many contractors post a generic cover letter as a response to job postings they are interested in. I NEVER hire contractors who won't put a personalized response in their application letter.

In order to weed out a bunch of people that I don't want, I state in my job posting, "Please include your favorite food in your response so I know that you read the entire posting." Then I only look at those responses that followed my instructions. You can usually weed out over 50% of the applicants this way. If they won't even read my job posting, they are certainly not working for me!

Monitor And Manage The Work

Once you have selected the contractor and started giving them work, communicate what you want done in a LOT of detail. They are human beings and will have their own ideas, perspectives, and will even make assumptions unconsciously when the detail is not clear enough. There is no harm in over-communicating.

Then check-in periodically. One of the most effective things you can do is to monitor progress along the way. For example, if you are having the same task done 100 times, ask the contractor to do the first ten and then let you take a look. That will give you a chance to provide feedback or input. Maybe you will realize that you don't want it done exactly the way you said! That's OK too. We are human and sometimes we need to see what we are asking for before we can decide if we like it or not.

Finally, remember that YOU are in charge. You make the calls and you make the final decisions. There will be contractors who think that they are in charge because of their unique or specialized perspective. Don't forget that YOU are the one who is orchestrating the entire thing; what you say goes. Sometimes specialists get caught up in the details and philosophy of their specialty area and do not have the larger perspective that you have. Don't tolerate that; you are the boss.

It's Never Going To Be Perfect

There is a sacrifice to be made when systematizing and outsourcing. The work will never be as good, as effective, or as much as it would be if you did everything yourself. That is a simple fact. You will need to accept this fact. But don't view it as a bad thing.

Leverage Is Worth The Hassle

What's happening is that you are creating leverage. Leverage makes your business do more than it could otherwise. The automatic systems will introduce some additional ways that things can get messed up. For example, during a recent software changeover I had a situation where a small number of customers who had purchased a product were sent an email sequence that attempted to sell it to them again. That was a bit embarrassing and annoying, but it is just a fact of life. The downside or damage done from that is far *less* than the limitations of *not having* an automated system.

I'm not saying to throw quality out the window. Quality is absolutely an important value in my business and in yours. You must focus on the things that matter the most. Put more emphasis on the quality of the actual products you create and the services you provide — as opposed to dotting all the i's and crossing all the t's.

I know you take a lot of pride in what you do and I applaud you for that. At the same time, don't limit yourself by being overly-focused on quality to the degree that it causes you more harm than good — that limits both the degree of success you can have and the amount of freedom you will have in your life.

Conclusion

This stuff is really important. People and processes are two of the most important aspects of an expert lifestyle business. Why? Because having the right people and processes in your business:

1. Frees you, the expert, to do the things that matter most to you, and
2. Allows your business to scale — meaning it can get as large (and make as much money) as you desire.

I recognize that people and processes aren't very exciting. It's not much fun to hire people, pay them, train them, and write business processes — at least it's not for me. However, I learned in my corporate career that you must make it a priority.

When I managed large projects and programs, I would generally start a new one every six to 18 months. Each time I started a new project there would be new staff and many new processes and procedures to be developed. The way I looked at it was that I could spend a day creating and staffing a process that would save me ten hours of work each week, OR I could spend the eight hours doing eight hours of work. The choice is obvious.

Those eight hours you spend training and systematizing are an eight-hour investment in getting you back to doing the things you most enjoy. View it as an investment in your happiness and in your business!

Think Of It Like This:

✗ There is nothing in your business more precious than your time.

✗ Develop a process mindset. They set you free.

✗ Processes are like a train that you build to move your business along. Once you've got the train rolling, just put fuel in it and couple on as many cars as you want.

✗ People are what will allow you to grow your business as large (and profitable) as you want it to be and provide you the freedom you want in life.

Do It Like This:

✓ Take the TIME to build processes and find good people to execute them. Commit to this as though your business and freedom depend on it —because they do.

✓ Create a leveraged, efficient lead process.

✓ Document the things that need to be done in your business as if you are writing it for a sixth grader, and identify the lowest skill set that could possibly do each of the steps.

✓ Find good people, pay them, and treat them well.

Chapter 11

Keep Up The Momentum

"Patience, persistence and perspiration make an unbeatable combination for success."
— Napoleon Hill

You've accomplished something awesome and truly amazing. You have now drawn your blueprints, cemented the foundation of your expert lifestyle business, erected your structure by creating deep connections with your followers, and erected your spire by creating and selling products and services to those followers. You may have sold less than 100 bucks worth of products and services, or perhaps you have sold tens of thousands. Either way, you've gotten started.

The amazing thing about selling that first product, whether it is a 97 cent Kindle e-book or a $5000.00 consulting package, is that you have done it. You have sold at least one. You have done it once — now you know that you can do it again and again and again.

The Feeling Of Freedom

What an incredible feeling this is — the freedom of being able to do whatever you want. You have proven to yourself that you can sell, and now you have the confidence that it's possible. You know you can do it over and over again to create the life you desire.

I talk a lot about the importance of knowing your followers and your target customers or prospects. I make that my absolute number one priority. I know my prospects, followers, and customers. Almost everything I do contains a component that is intended to get to know my followers better. That is why I can make the following statement confidently:

You are in this for the long haul; you are not looking for a get-rich-quick scheme. You are looking to build a lifestyle of freedom, and you love the fact that you can do something you care about. If you wanted a get-rich-quick scheme, you would have read a different book. This book is NOT positioned or written to appeal to people who want a get-rich-quick scheme. It is positioned and written for YOU. And if, for some reason, a person looking for a get-rich-quick scheme picked up this book, they would have stopped reading it long before now.

Take It To The Next Level

I know you want to keep up the momentum, and to keep building your business. That's what this chapter is about — taking your expert lifestyle business to the next level, growing relationships with your followers to a whole new level (beyond making the first sale), and taking your business to completely new heights.

It's All About Getting The Customer

First let's look at the concept of customers. It has been said that it costs five or six times more to get a new customer than to sell to an existing customer.

Therefore, my number one goal is to GET that customer. Why? Because I know it is the most valuable asset I can have. I believe it is so valuable that I don't care if I make money on that first sale!

What I want from the first sale is to *get a customer*. Not to get money. Once I get that customer, I know I will be able to make more money by selling him/her additional products and services.

Making Money Is Not The Goal On The First Sale

What do I mean when I say I don't care about making money on the first sale? Once I have that customer, I have the OPPORTUNITY to provide immense value to them and to make them happy as a clam. I have the OPPORTUNITY to make them love what I offer even more.

I KNOW that what I offer will make them love me; because what I provide is a great, high-quality product and will give them something they have been looking for for a while.

By the way, I generally DO make money on the first sale, from a pure unit-cost perspective. But that is not the goal. My goal is get a customer who is hugely satisfied and is so happy that they will put me at the top of their list for people they want to do business with.

It doesn't mean that the first product is cheap. It doesn't necessarily mean that it is hugely discounted either. The first product provides TONS of value for the amount paid; and I'm willing to spend a lot of money to make that first transaction a very successful one for both of us.

This whole mentality won't work for pure "internet marketers" or for the "get-rich-quick" people. Their businesses are not structured for the long haul, and they wouldn't be willing to delay making a profit for the long-term success and viability of their company. However, those of us creating expert lifestyle businesses are in it for the long haul, and will be perfectly happy to delay profits in exchange for much bigger things in the future.

Your Gateway Product

I borrowed this term from the concept of a gateway drug, which is a drug that generally leads to the use of other, more dangerous drugs. That's kind of a strange analogy, but it is basically the same concept; only here we're using it for good, instead of evil!

As you build your product suite, the products will get more and more expensive as your customers move up the ladder. You could start with a $97 video course and move up the scale to a $25,000 year-long program.

For example, if that first product is $97, I'm saying you should spend at least $97 (or more) to get that customer. There are a lot of ways you can do this:

Offer Generous Affiliate Commission

I offer a 50% commission on almost every product I sell. I would never create a product at this tier without designing it so that it can be sold with that level of commission. I intentionally do this because I don't want to be in a position where I can't offer that amount of commission. It's important to be generous with commissions, particularly on your gateway product. In other words, I'm building the ability to offer a 50% commission into the pricing structure.

I've never done it, but I would consider doing more than 50% commission in the right situation. That might be a viable option for you as well.

Spend Money On Your Prospects

As you've probably figured out by now, I'm not afraid of spending money to acquire prospects. Below are a few ways that I spend money to get customers and I highly recommend that you do some of these as well.

Use Paid Advertising

Paid advertising can be very effective. You do need to be careful. I have lost a LOT of money on paid advertising simply because it was not effective. Rather than jumping into Facebook ads, Google ads, sponsorships or other things like that, I highly recommend that you read a good book on the topic, get training, or hire someone to do it for you. Paid advertising is one area where I simply do not desire to acquire the detailed knowledge, so I choose to partner with others who do.

Live Events

I attend a considerable number of live events. At first, a large percentage of my prospects came from these events. However, it costs money to travel to and attend these events, but again, for me it has been worth it. In my particular niche, there are a number of events and conferences I can attend where I can connect with a large number of prospects. Frequently, I take along copies of my CD or book to give away to prospects who appear to be interested in my services.

Be Multi-Modal

I am a huge believer in being "multi-modal," which means being in front of people in a variety of modes. I accomplish that in many ways, but my favorite is using the good old-fashioned post office. I have a letter that gets sent out to prospects as soon as I acquire their mailing address. This might be sent to someone whose business card I received at a networking event or to an online lead if they provided their mailing address (or we were able to locate it).

The nice thing about my niche is that my prospects are frequently business owners, coaches or consultants, so a mailing address is pretty easy to obtain through a quick internet search. I also send an introductory letter to all paying customers, and most of my other product sales result in an introductory letter being sent as well.

I also frequently send my audio CD to prospects. I have this CD set up with Kunaki (kunaki.com). Once it is set up, I can ship either a single CD to an address or I can ship a large box of any number of CDs for events or promotional offers. When I ship a single copy of the CD, it costs me about $5.20 to have it created and shipped. Certainly every person who I ship a complimentary copy of this CD to will not buy from me, but the expense is well worth it.

Promotional Products

Promotional products are anything selling for less than about 25 bucks; and they are generally sold in order to get your information out there in an easily-digestible format, at a low price point. They include items such as a book, e-book, CD, DVD or other information product. Again, I view these as promotional tools that have the added benefit of possibly making a small amount of money. However, I want to be clear that I don't consider someone who has purchased a $15 book to be on the same level/tier as a customer who has purchased a $100 product.

You can also use promotional products as loss leaders; in other words, you can ship a complimentary copy of your book, or a single CD, or your audio series to prospective customers. This is yet another way to spend money to earn that first sale from the customer.

Make Them Happy The First Time

When someone throws down cash for your product, it's your job to ensure that they get nothing less than the most awesome, amazing experience you can possibly deliver. This is true ANYTIME a customer pays money, but is particularly crucial on this first purchase.

This is the first time they are "in your house." Just like interior designers who talk about the importance of the foyer or entryway in making a first impression, your first product must leave your prospects with a memorable, value-packed first impression.

Bring In Other Experts For Added Value

Consider creative ideas such as bringing in additional guest experts (your peers, who you have been developing relationships with) to deliver part of this product. Perhaps you know a colleague who has knowledge that is complementary to yours and would benefit your customer. Consider paying that person a portion of the sales for their contribution to the product. Yes, that is cutting into your profit; but that's OK because it is making that first experience that the customer has that much more awesome and valuable. The goal is to make them more likely to buy the second product!

Provide A Physical Product

In our modern, online world we are too quick to overlook providing physical media to our customers. I provide something physical in the mail for most purchases. There is cost involved, but it's not that much and it does a lot to separate you from your competitors who might be delivering in bits and bytes (electronic-only products).

Provide An Opportunity For Interaction

Consider including some type of live interaction as a feature of your products. In this day and age of information overload, people crave live interaction. This could be a 30 minute one-on-one; it could be a group call; or it might even be some sort of live event, if your price point allows it. Don't discount this as an option.

Build Your Product Suite Upward

I never sell a single product without having an upsell in mind. By upsell, I'm not talking about a "do you want fries with that" approach. I'm referring to another product in the pipeline that you want to sell to the customer. For example, when customers have completed a $97 online training, they may sold into a six-week coaching program, priced at $997.00.

The reality is that you will not have a follow-on product for every single customer, because technically it would require an infinite number of products! The point is that you should shoot for that ideal. You want to work toward having a product suite of at least six products, starting with a book or CD for less than 20 bucks, and having tiers all the way up into the thousands of dollars.

The price of these products is dependent upon your topic and niche. Do the research on your niche. If there are no $2000 products available, then there is probably a reason. It could be an untapped market, but that's not likely. It's best to stay inside the range of what others are doing in your niche. Since we've spent most of our efforts so far building up a following, you now have the luxury of being able to ask your followers what they would pay for something! Also, you have built a network of peers in your topic area, so you can get their ideas and perspectives as well.

Conclusion

That is the stuff that takes your business to the next level. This is exactly what sends your expert lifestyle business to awesome new places and puts you on the path toward creating your life of freedom. It is a great thing that we can do as much as we can today for free, or at least inexpensively, but in order to take your business to the level you want, spend money to obtain leads and spend money to give your paying customers an amazing, unforgettable experience.

Think Of It Like This:

×   This is not a get-rich-quick program; you are in it for the long haul.

×   The first sale to a customer is the most important. Once they have bought (at any price point), you have the opportunity to sell them more products from your product suite.

×   Customers are your most valuable asset. Treat them like gold and they will continue to buy from you.

Do It Like This:

✓   Spend as much money to obtain the customer as you will make on your gateway product.

✓   Create an integrated suite of products; so that each time someone buys there is another product that will allow them to go further with you.

✓   Be multi-modal. Don't rely solely on free or low-cost digital methods to promote your business.

Chapter 12

Harness Your Freedom

"Seek freedom and become captive of your desires. Seek discipline and find your liberty."
— Frank Herbert

I remember the first week after I left my job. I had planned a LOT of things to do for my business that week. I had also put off running a lot of errands, like going to the bank, post office, etc. I put them off because I thought it would be so much easier to do them once I was no longer working my full-time job.

I took that first Wednesday morning and got caught up on a bunch of those errands and miscellaneous stuff. And that was great. I got a taste of flexibility and loved it. That is a small example, but for me it was symbolic of what I was creating.

The Best And The Worst

The best things about having an expert lifestyle business are:

- You have complete control of how you schedule and spend your time.
- You have complete control of how much money you make.
- You can play whatever roles you want to in your business.

However, I realized that while this was the most awesome thing I'd ever done for myself, it still was not going to be easy. The biggest thing that I had to come to grips with was that time was STILL not as abundant as I thought it was going to be!

I have gotten clear on what I want my life to look like and I understand what it will take to make it that way. Not working a full-time job has made it so much easier to move in that direction, but it has also created some challenges.

The most dangerous aspects of having an expert lifestyle business are:

- You have complete control of how you schedule and spend your time.
- You have complete control of how much money you make.
- You can play whatever roles you want to in your business.

Did you notice the lists are exactly the same? The best parts of an expert lifestyle business are also the worst. The great thing is that it comes down to control. YOU have control of just about everything — and that is awesome. But like anything, you can either make it great or you can screw it up.

Complete Control Over Your Schedule

How amazing! You now get to choose exactly how to spend your time; you set your schedule; you decide when you have meetings, when you work and when you don't. There is no need to fit your schedule into any type of mold.

Create Your Ideal Schedule

I love that I get to make my schedule whatever I want it to be. At first, I thought I still needed to fit into some sort of mold. For example, I thought I needed to get up at 7:30 AM each day and start working immediately. I tried that for a while; it didn't work out so well. It didn't work out mainly because I'm NOT a morning person. I eventually backed off of that notion and started getting up later and taking the time that I need in the morning to wake up and get "in the zone" before I start working. That works out much better for me.

You get to completely control your schedule. You get to work the hours you want to, not the hours that someone else wants you to.

Mondays Are Fun!

When I worked in the corporate world, like most people, Mondays were AWFUL! I hated Mondays. Now I make sure to do my favorite activities on Mondays. It's the coolest thing, and has enabled me to take something that used to be a negative and turn it into a positive.

I also have always enjoyed being off on Sundays, so I kept that schedule. Sunday is the only non-negotiable day for me. Nobody gets Sunday — it's mine. There are plenty other times that are not generally available for work, but they are more negotiable than Sundays.

Some might say there is a danger that this lifestyle might cause you to not work ENOUGH. While that is true for some people, that generally isn't an issue for committed entrepreneurs. I doubt it's true of people who have read this far in this book. Rather than talk about that, let's address the opposite side of the coin — working too much.

Time Off Is Valuable

It helped me immensely when I thought about it differently — I began to view the time I spent away from my business as being as important as the time I spent working on my business. That was a huge turning point for me. I stopped thinking of myself as being naughty when I wasn't working on my business. The time I spend away is just as important as the time I spend working! Why? Because it recharges me and helps me feel well-rested and inspired so I can bring my fullest to the business. I know that sounds basic, and that it's probably written in about 70,000 self-help books, but actually viewing the situation that way is completely another story. Time off is important. Don't rob yourself of the benefit you've created.

Complete Control Of Money

If you are making lots of money, you get all the credit. If you are not making any (or enough) money, it's your fault. There is no blaming your stupid boss who doesn't appreciate you, the HR pay scales, or anyone else but you! I think that's a good thing. When I worked in the corporate world, I could have moved heaven and earth, and even if I did that successfully, there was only so much money I was ever going to get paid.

Not so when you have your own expert lifestyle business. If you do amazing things in your expert lifestyle business, you will get compensated in amazing ways. I love being completely and totally in charge of my own destiny. It's the most awesome, freeing feeling ever.

On the other hand, if you don't do the right things, don't do enough, or have the wrong mindset, you will not make money, will not enjoy your life, and will not be happy or free. Don't despair though; the good news is that you now know exactly what to do! You are in the driver's seat and know the map to follow.

Play Whatever Roles You Want To

It's totally up to you. You can write computer code; you can lead seminars; you can handle customer support; you can write books — it's all up to you. What will matter most is what you do and do not decide to do yourself.

That's a great thing. I cannot emphasize this enough:

> YOU GET TO DO WHAT YOU WANT TO DO, AND YOU DON'T HAVE TO DO WHAT YOU DON'T WANT TO DO!

I friggin' love this business!

What other situations in life are dictated by what you want? Not many other than birthdays! Every day is your birthday now.

Do What You Love

Decide what parts of your business are your favorites and do them. Do them and enjoy them. Then look at the parts you don't like, and don't do them. Hire someone and get back to doing what you want to do.

Always ask yourself what YOU bring to your expert lifestyle business. YOU are the centerpiece of the business and it's very important that you showcase YOUR assets! You are not showcasing YOUR assets by updating the database, resetting passwords, scheduling meetings, or anything like that. It's your job to get out there and get known by talking to people, creating content and delivering products.

Embrace Your Freedom!

The biggest mistake I made when I stopped working was that I didn't EMBRACE my new life. I did not fully step into it because I thought I needed to get to some magical place before I could. I didn't feel like I deserved freedom until I got to a certain point. I had a few people in my life (both paid consultants) that encouraged me to step into my new lifestyle. I thank them sincerely for the strong encouragement they gave me to step into and embrace the life I had created for myself.

This was amazing. It allowed me to embody this whole life of freedom on a new level, and that set off a chain reaction of great things that started happening. I had to get over the concept that there was some magical milestone or point that made it OK to finally enjoy the life I had created.

A good thing can only be a good thing if you let it be. You can let this amount of freedom take you to the most amazing heights imaginable or you can let it drag you down to the lowest depths you can fathom.

Having A Business Is Harder

I haven't sugar-coated anything in this book and I'm sure not going to start now. It really is harder to have a business of your own than it is to work for someone else. There is absolutely no guarantee that you will make money next month. If you do, there's no guarantee it will be more than what you spent. There is no built-in discipline either. There's no one to bust you for sleeping on the job or playing hooky. That makes self-discipline a MUST.

It's a simple matter of responsibility. With no one else to blame, you must take complete and total responsibility for everything that does or does not happen.

When you are doing what you absolutely love more than anything, and you are doing it HOW you love to do it, you are all set. You are in the best place you can be.

For Goodness Sake, Do It

As hard as it is for me to admit (and it is hard), this lifestyle is not for everyone. But if you are concerned that it's not for YOU, think again. You wouldn't have read this far if it wasn't for you. You probably see challenges. You are probably thinking "yeah but..." and filling in the biggest thing that worries you. Things like:

"Yeah, but I have a family to take care of." So do most of my clients. I don't have kids, but I can't imagine a better thing to do for them than to demonstrate that you value your life enough to take control of it. INVALID

"Yeah, but I don't know enough about my topic (or anything) to actually make money." This is true in some cases, but not in most. Either a) you aren't giving yourself enough credit or b) you just need to learn more, and there is no better or easier time to learn than right now. INVALID

"Yeah, but I don't have time to do all this work." First I'd have to challenge you on that. How much time do you spend each week being entertained? If it's hard to imagine giving up TV, think of it this way: what if you were doing something you enjoyed more than TV? If you still can't find enough time, take whatever time you have. The Lifestyle Masterplan™ is very flexible, in that you can work on it a little at a time, and build slowly if necessary. INVALID

I could list 100 of these. The bottom line is that they are all excuses. You have to make a decision and a commitment and stick to it. If you have read this far, it is my duty to challenge you in a big way.

Step Up

It is time for you to step up. You have read over 50,000 words about how to create the life of your dreams using your knowledge — that tells me there is a ton of potential inside you. Not to mention, this book probably isn't the first thing you've read on the topic, and I certainly hope it's not the last.

You deserve to live the life of your dreams. You deserve to have the life of freedom that you desire.

If you don't think you deserve it, consider the people you could help. Do they deserve the benefit of the knowledge you offer?

Part of the mission statement for my company is:

> *"to change the way people who need knowledge are connected with the people who have the knowledge."*

This is in the mission statement because I want my company to make a difference in the world (in many different ways) and that's how we're going to do it. You have knowledge and people need that knowledge. My company's mission is to connect you with them. Everything we do is toward the goal of creating that connection. At this very moment, my job is to convince you to GET OUT THERE! Get out there and DO IT!

Why not?

Why wouldn't you? I'm offering you the chance of a lifetime.

- Have all the freedom you've ever wanted, both in terms of money and time.
- Do something you really care about and enjoy doing more than anything else.
- Make a difference in the world with your knowledge.

What is the problem? I can't see the downside!

You Are The Solution

There are a lot of problems in the world now, but let's consider one. The education system in the US is failing miserably. It is failing nearly every child who goes through it. If we were to completely tear down what we call education today and start from scratch, the foundation of what we build would start with finding people who care deeply about and love a topic and pairing them up with those who need that knowledge. You are half of that equation. And you are the half that has the most control.

It is your job to identify what you have to offer, who needs that knowledge, and what problem or desire they have that your knowledge can address. Once you have done that, you are ready to start closing a gap and making a huge difference in the world.

It Doesn't Feel Like Work

If you are worried about the amount of work, stop worrying. When you love what you do, it's not work anymore. I'm writing this sitting on my sofa on New Year's Eve, and there is nothing else in the world I would rather be doing. That's why I called this book "How to Quit Working." It's not about *not doing* anything. It's about *doing* things that you love so much that it's not about "working" or "not working" anymore.

Final Word

Thanks for reading this book. It's the culmination of a lifetime of work, experience, research and training. I'm honored and humbled that you took the time to read it.

Life is too short — do what you want and be happy. That's all that really matters. I've given you an amazing foundation on which to build that life. Now it's your turn to make it so.

For more information and a a FREE video training series on creating a life of FREEDOM using your knowledge (along with other useful resources) please visit:

howtoquitworkingbook.com

Best Always,
Jeff Steinmann

ACKNOWLEDGMENTS

I would like to acknowledge the following people who directly or indirectly made this book possible.

Debra Steinmann is my mom and has put up with my crap longer than anyone else and has always been incredibly supportive. I love her very much despite her trying to pass off instant mashed potatoes as homemade on several occasions.

John Drake is one of my oldest friends and has had a profound influence on who I am today through our many late night philosophical discussions over cheap beer.

Dan Riordan who has put up with more of my crap than possibly anyone on the planet and supported *almost* all of my crazy, hair-brained schemes and edited this book.

Donald Stepps who has been so incredibly helpful and supportive throughout this entire process and someday will be a world renowned motivational speaker named Stepp Steppington.

Bill and Andrea Nickrent are my friends and neighbors who were available for many late night, hair-on-fire emergency consultations on this book and other aspects of my business.